180 DAYS TO SAVE THE WORLD

Write and Publish a Short Story Collection

Jane Garrett
with cover art by Christian Reid

Copyright © 2022 by Jane Garrett

All rights reserved. No part of this book may be reproduced or used in any manner by any electronic or mechanical means including information storage and retrieval systems without the prior written permission of the publisher, except for the use of brief quotations in a book review.

To request permissions, contact the publisher:
admin@innovativelearningpress.com

Distributed in the United States
Paperback: 978-1-7375557-4-2

First paperback edition September 2022.

Edited by Gill McDonald
Cover art by Christian Reid

Innovative Learning Press
Apache Junction, AZ
www.innovativelearningpress.com

Acknowledgments

Thank you to all of my former students. You are the reason I wanted to write these workbooks. Your enthusiasm to write your first novel sparked the desire in me to make sure you had all the tools you needed to become a young author. I want you to know that because of you; I am still guiding students to realize their dream of writing their own novels and short stories.

I would like to thank the many authors who have inspired and equipped me with the knowledge and advice I needed to complete this project. Your wisdom and insight have been a tremendous guide and I pray you continue to write, teach, and influence aspiring authors to connect with readers through emotional storytelling.

I especially want to thank my kiddos, Emma and Christian. For all the unwavering support and believing that mom could do "anything." Even though you are now "grown," you still believe I am a superhero. I love you for that.

Most of all, thank you Captain Awesome! You have always believed in me and your support is the main reason I continued to torture myself week after week, hunched over my computer. Remember when you told me it would be worth it? As sometimes happens, you were right. You cleaned house, scrounged dinner, walked the dog, did the dishes, and made sure I had everything I needed to complete another writing project. I would not have been able to accomplish this without your full support. I am so glad you married me.

TABLE OF CONTENTS

1. **Getting Started**   **1**

    a. Using this Workbook
    b. Author's Toolkit
    c. What is a Short Story
    d. Your Story
    e. Why Outline?

2. **Generate Your Idea**   **13**

    a. Your Big Idea
    b. Plot
    c. POV
    d. Your Premise

3. **Story Elements**   **27**

    a. Five elements of story
    b. Character
    c. The Others
    d. Story Goal
    e. Setting
    f. Conflict
    g. Theme

4. **Getting Organized**   **81**

    a. A General Sketch
    b. Your Outline
    c. Starting Strong
    d. Scene Breaks

TABLE OF CONTENTS

5. Writing Mechanics   **93**

     a. The Illusion of Reality
     b. Three Modes of Fiction
     c. Adverbs
     d. Cliché
     e. Passive Voice

6. Writing Your Story   **111**

     a. Writing the Draft
     b. Your Internal Editor
     c. Formatting

7. The Revision Process   **115**

     a. Revising your Draft
     b. Tips for Self-Revising
     c. Critique Partner
     d. Publishing Short Stories

8. Self-Publishing   **119**

     a. Self-Publishing a Collection
     b. Formatting a Collection
     c. Front & Back Matter
     d. Front Cover
     e. Back Cover
     f. The Final Step

9. Bonus Materials   **125**

CHAPTER ONE

Getting Started

Using this Workbook

Welcome to the 180 *Days to Save the World* short story writing course. This workbook is set up so that you can learn, brainstorm, make mistakes, and create an amazing story! I want to stress the mistakes part of that. Planning any story will have you going back over previous ideas and making changes based on new ideas and lessons learned from this book. If you are a student who doesn't like "messy" pages, I suggest now is a good time to reconsider that. Creating something amazing is usually messy.

With that in mind, you might want to fill your brainstorming parts out in pencil so you can erase and rewrite things. I have given you enough room to write, but you can always add pages by just stapling them to an existing page. Consider this workbook to be like a scrapbook. The scrappier it looks, the more personal and filled with "you" it will be.

Just know that this is a *work*book. It is meant to be worked over and over. Make changes, and do not be afraid to wipe out entire sections or plot ideas and start fresh if it feels right. Give yourself the freedom to do that because I guarantee that if you really want to write the best short story you can, you must accept that you will scratch entire ideas and scenes you have already written for better ones.

There are extra pages on which to take notes based on your research and ideas, and you can paste clippings from magazines, newspapers, or other sources that you may want to refer to. It will truly become your scrapbook for adventure.

I will often refer to the protagonist as "he," just to make it simple, but obviously, besides gender, heroes come in all sizes and shapes. Even species. Since this workbook series is geared towards adventure novels, the protagonist will often be referred to as the "hero."

Last, be prepared to work. Many students underestimate the volume of details that go into writing a story. There are rules and formats that must be followed. It takes more than just a good idea. Be prepared to immerse yourself in the lessons and reach deep inside to that imaginative place that we were all created with. Be honest and open with emotions, and never, ever think any idea is stupid. If it is truly honest, then readers will relate to it.

Author's Toolkit

It is important that as I am talking and giving instructions, you understand what I am saying. Many of my words may be new to you. I think the best way to start is to learn some common terms that we will use throughout this course.

Look up all the words listed below and write the definition. If there is more than one definition listed for a word, make sure you refer to the literary definition, that is, the one having to do with books and stories.

1. Protagonist-

2. Antagonist-

3. Fiction-

4. Genre-

5. Manuscript-

6. Draft-

7. Freewrite-

8. Scene-

9. Narrative-

10. Climax-

11. Plot-

12. Sub-plot-

13. Setting-

14. Theme-

15. Point-of-View-

16. Conflict-

17. Cliché-

18. Synopsis-

19. Character Arc-

20. Serif Font-

What is a Short Story?

Stories come in all lengths and sizes. There is some conflicting information, but a general rule for story length is that stories longer than 10,000 but shorter than 40,000 words long are usually considered novellas, a novelette refers to a story between 7,500 and 17,000 words long, and once you hit about 40,000 words, you're in novel territory, starting with chapter books.

Stories that have less than 1,000 words are known as flash fiction, and stories with less than 500 words are called micro-fiction. The latter is very popular in school in-class writing assignments based on writing prompts.

However, there's really no limit to how short a story can be. Ernest Hemingway once bet a bunch of fellows he could make them cry with a short story six words long. If he won the bet, each guy would have to pay him ten dollars. Hemingway's six-word story was, "For sale: Baby shoes, never worn." He won the bet.

In just six words, Hemingway evokes an entire scene and the backstory that led to that scene. This is an extreme example of micro-fiction, and it relies on the reader taking meaning from the words, but because it does so successfully, it counts as a story.

Short stories are not novels, but they have the same elements of plot, character, setting, and theme. They usually have 1,000 - 10,000 words and are often easier for new writers to manage than a full-length novel. Short stories are to novels what television shows are to movies. Short and to the point with plenty of action and characters that readers love.

Because of the shortened length, short stories are less complex than novels. In a short story, you can have multi-dimensional characters, but you can't go into backstory and meaningful character arcs like you can in a longer story. Similarly, you can build your world, but not to the extent you would do in a novel. Intricate plots and multiple sub-plots are not included in a short story, but you can still have a main plot that really packs a punch.

One of the best ways you can learn to write a great short story is to first read some short stories. This is a very important step. Many websites have short stories online that you can read for free. You can also visit your local library and check out a book of short stories. Physical books will not contain a single short story but a collection of short stories gathered under one title.

Short stories can also be categorized by the target age of the reader. Children's, middle grade, young adult (YA), and adult are popular categories in fiction. These are often confused with literature genres, but they are not. They are considered categories.

You will keep a log of the short stories that you read and what you liked or did not like about them. This step will help you develop your story. I have provided a reading log table for you on the next page.

TITLE & AUTHOR	STORY SUMMARY

Your Story

There is what is referred to as genre fiction, and then there is literary fiction. Genre fiction is a type of story that has a more mainstream appeal than literary fiction. Genre fiction is traditionally composed of the main genres of romance, mystery, thriller, science fiction (sci-fi), fantasy, YA, speculative, and historical fiction. Young adult (YA) is considered a category, like middle grade or adult, but it is also often spoken of as being its own genre for novels.

Most great stories combine two or more of these genres to be successful. Having a touch of romance in your fantasy story is very popular. In fact, many books of all genres contain a touch of romance. It is considered a sub-plot. You can also have a historical fiction that is sci-fi, like a travel back in time story. Either way, it's good to understand genres, but don't limit yourself.

You can write your short story in any genre that you choose. For the purpose of this curriculum, we will often refer to the literary sub-genre adventure. Adventure fiction is a literary sub-genre featuring exciting tales of catastrophes, heroes, villains, and risk-filled journeys. You do not have to write a specific adventure story, but in some ways, all stories are adventures.

For your story, I will offer you some good writing advice that I know is most helpful for new writers. Write what you know. You should write about a character that is close to your age. This can relate to gender and circumstance as well, but it is just a writing tool so that you can focus more on story development and less on researching a character type of which you have little personal experience. This does not mean that you cannot have a protagonist that is completely different from you. It's just a suggestion. Your character does not even have to be human. It can be an animal or other species, like many popular stories use.

You will write in the YA category, which means your audience is in their teen years. The minimum count is 3,000 words. This is a good starting point for your first self-published fiction piece. Outside of that, you can write about whatever you want. Just remember, when we make references to adventure or heroes, it is just a point of reference. This is your story, and you will make it uniquely your own.

Why Outline?

There are many different methods of writing a story. Some authors are called "Pantsers." They just write their story without having any idea of which direction it will take or what will happen. They make it up as they go along. The term comes from "flies by the seat of their pants," which is defined as "to rely on instinct rather than logic or knowledge." Most authors are not Pantsers. It is very difficult to write without planning, and only a very few are successful with that method.

The other types of authors are referred to as "Plotters." They plot all the elements and chapters of their entire story before writing anything. They plan their characters in extensive detail, every chapter's action, and even how they want the reader to react. It's all a part of their planning process. This process is referred to as outlining your story.

This curriculum uses outlining. As an author myself, I cannot even get motivated to write a story before I complete a lot of research and then outline all the different elements. For short stories, the outlining may not be as detailed as a 70,000-word novel, but it will involve planning. Let's look at the reasons outlining is important.

First, most Pantsers will tell you they are not organized people and are just so creative that they have to sit down and write. Very few writers can do that and stay on track without missing details or going far off course. The revision process is brutal. Pantsers can end up throwing out sections and even entire chapters that they spent weeks writing because they did not fit when they looked at the completed story.

For those who outline, here are some of the main reasons why:

1. It will help avoid writer's block. It's quite common for writers who use the Pantser method to start their story with great enthusiasm but then reach a point where they don't know how to continue. Knowing how the plot will advance will make it much easier to finish your story.

2. You'll always know what you need to write. By having an event timeline for your story, you'll know what is coming next. This will make the process go faster because you will not sit around thinking too much about what needs to happen. You just write.

3. You can focus on what's important. If you have good planning, when you work on your first draft, you can concentrate on enjoying the story. You'll be able to focus all your energy on creating scenes that make the setting, conflict, dialogue, and characters really stand out.

4. Your revision process will be easier. If your story is outlined, then it will be a smooth transition from scene to scene and will be very consistent in all the elements.

5. You can be more creative. It might seem the opposite, but more planning ahead allows you to be more creative. It's like having a map when you take a road trip. Your GPS app tells you where to go so that if you decide to stop somewhere and have a little fun, your app will redirect you back on the path and get you to your destination. You can get as creative with your scenes as you want because your outline will always get you back on track.

Outlining is a powerful writer's tool to make sure your amazing story is well written so the reader can relax and enjoy the journey you will take them on. Even if you are writing a short story, outlining the main events, conflicts, and character arcs will ensure that you stay on point with rising action to a satisfying finish.

I want to make sure you understand there is a difference between brainstorming and outlining. Brainstorming methods help you narrow down what your book is about as well as sketch out an idea of your characters and setting. Even with all those great ideas and notes you have, it is still not the same as outlining your story. **A story outline includes important information about the structure, plot, characters, scenes, and more.** It is the skeleton of your story laid out. It functions as your roadmap.

There are different methods for outlining stories, but most of them apply to writing novels or chapter books. Not all have official names, and no one method is necessarily better than another. A lot depends on the kind of story you are writing and your own personality. Some people combine more than one method.

For this curriculum, we will use the traditional outlining method, sometimes referred to as a general sketch. This will be based on your brainstorming that we will do together in the next chapter.

Before we move forward with traditional outlining, let's practice what this looks like for short stories. You will do this by taking an existing short story and reverse engineering it into an outline. Read a story and write a basic summary paragraph and then list the key events.

To ensure that you work with enough variety of stories, do this for at least three different short stories but I encourage you to do more. Make sure you read from different authors and, if possible, different genres. Use the worksheet on the following page to give a basic outline of the story. Think in terms of key events, like a timeline, and write them as a list. This is not a summary of a story, it is a general sketch of the events that happen in the story.

TITLE

OUTLINE

TITLE

OUTLINE

CHAPTER TWO

Your Story

Your Big Idea

Original vs. Unique:

A fictional story is simply a long, drawn-out lie meant to entertain and twist us into knots that keep us turning pages until we're unknotted. Fiction is like all art; it is very subjective. That means that art is based on personal preferences. However, one thing that can be said for certain is that there is no such thing as an original storyline.

Don't worry; it's okay. There are only so many possible storylines like boy meets girl, someone travels through time, a stranger comes to town, a guy sets off on a noble quest, and so on. Therefore, don't worry about coming up with an original story idea. **What you are looking to write is not something original but something unique.**

To understand the difference better, look up the definition of these two words and write it here:

Original-

Unique-

A unique story means you can simply take a storyline that has already been done before and put your own spin on it. It's going to differ from the original because of the characters you create, how you write, and the twists and turns you put into the story. In other words, you are telling the same old story in a cool new way.

You can do that by adding a twist to an old tale. Cinderella is one of the best examples. Scholars disagree as to exactly how many versions of the popular fairy tale exist, with numbers ranging from 340 to over 3,000. These figures include picture books and musical interpretations. But either way, this story has been told over and over in many new and interesting ways.

Whether your short story is an adaptation of a classic story or a unique version of a typical plot, it must have characters we care about doing things we could only dream of. They will face giants and legends, get defeated and come back bruised but not destroyed. Remember that your readers are teenagers. They have vivid imaginations. To a young adult, the line between reality and imagination is pretty blurred. You can create amazing stories that will be sure to keep your readers hooked.

Let's practice taking something borrowed and turning it into something new. Take three classic stories or scenes from a story (book or movie) and put your own twist on it.

Write a one-paragraph summary for each new plot idea:

Story - _____

New Plot Idea:

Story - _____

New Plot Idea:

Story - _____

New Plot Idea:

Plot

In Chapter One, you wrote the definitions of many common literary terms. Remember that a plot represents the events that make up a story or the main part of a story. In its simplest form, a plot is what happens in a story. A plot comes complete with rising action, a climax, and a resolution of the story goal.

According to author Margaret Atwood, there are seven basic plot types in genre writing, namely tragedy, comedy, hero's journey, rags to riches, rebirth, overcoming a monster, and voyage and return.

However, remember that I said writing is art and is therefore subjective? There are actually many more plot types, depending on who you ask. The following is a list I have compiled from multiple sources:

1. Tragedy
2. Rebirth
3. Person versus self
4. Person versus person
5. Person versus society
6. Person versus nature
7. Person versus the supernatural
8. Person versus technology
9. Quest
10. Adventure
11. Pursuit
12. Rescue
13. Escape
14. Revenge
15. The riddle
16. Rivalry
17. Underdog
18. Temptation

19. Metamorphosis

20. Transformation

21. Maturation

22. Love

23. Forbidden love

24. Sacrifice

25. Discovery

26. Wretched excess

27. Deliverance

28. Crime pursued by vengeance

29. Pursuit

30. Disaster

31. Falling prey to cruelty of misfortune

32. Revolt

33. Daring enterprise

34. Abduction

35. Obtaining

36. Enmity of kinsmen

37. Rivalry of kinsmen

38. Madness

39. Self-sacrifice for an ideal

40. Self-sacrifice for kindred

41. Rivalry between superior and inferior

42. Discovery of the dishonor of a loved one

43. An enemy loved

44. Ambition

45. Conflict with a God

46. Mistaken jealousy

47. Bad judgment

48. Remorse

49. Recovery of a lost one

50. Loss of loved ones

Most modern stories use a combination of plots, and you can choose anything that you want. This information is to help stimulate your brainstorming process.

When you create your plot in the next chapter, it will be important to understand that, in short stories, plots are pretty basic and straightforward. The really interesting part comes from the characters and how they defeat the many obstacles you will put in their way. All stories have the same basic elements, and you are free to create the type of plot that interests you most.

Select five different plots from the provided list, and next to it, write the title of books or movies that used that plot:

1.

2.

3.

4.

5.

Point of View (POV):

Besides the plot and character you start with, it is important to decide which point of view (POV) you will write from. POV is who is telling the story. With very few exceptions, every story is written in the first or third person. Let's take a closer look at each:

> First-Person (I): This is easier for beginners because there are no POV shifts, and it is more personal to describe what the protagonist is thinking when the protagonist is you. Readers can become connected with the character, making the emotional journey of the story easier for them. You cannot, however, know details that are going on outside of what the character personally sees or is told by someone else who was a witness. This means they must be present to know what happened somewhere, or someone who was present must tell them what happened.

> Third-person (he, she): In third-person, you can tell the reader things that the protagonist does not know or see himself. This allows the author to jump around from character to character, showing more of the story. You can still show the character's thoughts, but you need to be careful with shifting between different characters' POVs. You can do third-person writing from one character's perspective, like your protagonist, and it is recommended that, if you choose third-person, you only use your protagonist's perspective.

The POV you choose will have no material effect on how you will use this workbook. It is a matter of personal choice for what you find most helpful to tell your story. Regardless of which POV you choose to write in, you must pay attention to the rules outlined in the descriptions above. If you choose first-person, you cannot write about anything the hero does not witness personally or is not told by another character. If you write in third-person, you should only write from your hero's perspective.

To make this clear, if you write in first-person, you will be inside the hero's head and use "I," but if you choose third-person, you can talk about his thoughts, but you will always refer to him by name or "he." If you still don't understand, go back to some of your favorite stories and read through them. Pay attention to the POV they use. Are they referring to the character by name or "he/ she," or does it seem like the character is doing all the talking with "I" statements?

On the next page, you will free write a micro-fiction piece in the POV you have chosen, either first or third-person. You can write about anything you want, but it must be 350-500 words. This can even be an idea for your story you intend to write, and you can use it as practice.

Your Premise

By the time you sit down to outline your first story, you have most likely had one or more storylines chasing around in your head for some time, including characters, scenes, conflict, success, and so on; it's all there, somewhere. The first goal is to nail those thoughts down into what's referred to as a premise.

A premise is a single sentence that conveys a plot or theme. Don't worry, your premise may change several times throughout the outlining process, but it will help you get focused and narrow down your storyline. **The goal of your premise is to convey the character, setting, conflict, and story goal, all in one sentence.**

All stories start with a premise (an epic battle, two strangers falling in love, a spy being revealed to the enemy), and most premises start with the great "What if?" question:

> What if a little boy's brain grew too quickly for his body to keep up? *Ender's Shadow* by Orson Scott Card.
>
> What if siblings traveled to another world through a wardrobe? *The Chronicles of Narnia* by CS Lewis.
>
> What if a young woman fell in love with a paraplegic who plans to have himself euthanized? *Me Before You* by JoJo Moyes.

The power of the "What if?" question has produced many thousands of the most cherished stories. Whether or not you have an idea for your story, it is good to explore possibilities. Your "What if?" question can be a twist on an old tale or based on a plot type listed in the previous section.

Writing down every idea, no matter how "dumb" or insignificant they may seem, allows you to find the true gems that may end up becoming the greatest story ever written. Ready to brainstorm "What if?"

Let's take it a bit deeper now and talk about what is expected. All stories are cliché in some way. Every storyline that can be written has already been written by someone, somewhere. And guess what? It's okay because readers have expectations, and some of those need to be met. **Your job as an author is to give them something expected BUT in an unexpected way.**

For now, you are going to take your three "What if?" questions and ask, "What is expected?" In the example of Cinderella, it was expected that Cinderella would marry the prince and rise in station above her wicked stepmother. This process is crucial to understanding what it means to write a story that people will want to read. Now it's your turn to try.

Write your three favorite "What if?" questions, and beneath

Great job! Now, it's time to narrow these down to the most appealing idea and choose just one. From the "What if?" scenarios you wrote, which do you like best? What draws you and inspires the most ideas?

Of the three "What if?" and "What is expected?"

Now, we will turn the "What is expected?" you have selected over on its head. This is where the unexpected comes in. Readers love the unexpected! Remember when I said you must give them what is expected but in an unexpected way? This is the point where you shock and surprise your reader. You will twist your story in a way that will be unexpected but still fulfill the reader's expectations.

In the case of Cinderella, it was expected that she would marry the prince. Well, maybe she does marry, but it's not the prince. It's the prince's double, and he's really a servant. It was a sham put on by her evil stepmother. Can you imagine? Oh, the possibilities. Ultimately, she either needs to marry the prince, or the fake prince needs to be a better guy, and she gets everything she desires and more in the happily ever after. That is the idea.

Back to your "What is expected?" This is where you use your imagination again. Don't hold back; there are no foolish ideas and somewhere in that pile of creativity is a jewel of an idea. Go back to your selected "What if?" where you wrote out the "What is expected?" and use them to create surprise and tension in your story, a potential plot twist.

You have explored a lot of good ideas and are ready to write your premise. You must refine all the possibilities into a single, powerful premise. **Your "What if?" gives you an idea, but your premise gives you a story.**

Remember, your premise is a single sentence that conveys plot and theme. The breakdown of a successful premise is: Character - Story Goal - Opponent - Disaster.

Here are a few examples:

> After starting a mysterious board game, the players are sucked inside of it to break the curse, save the land, and find a way out before they die. *(Jumanji)*

> A man lives an idyllic life in a perfect community with the perfect family but longs for more, and when he finally attempts to leave his town, he finds out the entire thing is a reality show and everyone around him are just actors. *(The Truman Show)*

Now it's your turn to try. Write your premise statement and remember that the premise will not only identify an actual story but will also solidify character, plot, and conflict. Remember, your premise needs to hook someone's attention, or your book never will.

I realize you have not fleshed out your character or the theme yet, but you have a general idea. This premise is a working theory for your story. It's a place to start, and you are welcome to come back later and revise it as your story develops. Make sure you have the situation, character, story goal, opponent(s), and disaster all represented. Even though you are writing a short story, you will have all these elements in it since it is a complete story.

CHAPTER THREE

Story Elements

Five Elements of Story

There are five elements to every story, and you are going to work on them in-depth before you ever write a single page. These are commonly known as setting, character, plot, conflict, and theme. And while tradition holds that these are present in every story, we are going to look at these from a different viewpoint than some other traditional writing methods do.

For example, knowing you need a main character is not necessarily going to give you an interesting, dimensional, and even complex character that readers will not only remember but identify with. You must create a character that the reader will become emotionally invested in. The reader is then drawn to them and probably even identifies with them. That character is someone to care about.

In the same way, a plot is essentially a blueprint for your story, and most of you are familiar with that common reference in creative writing. It is what organizes the rising action and final resolution and is what many writing books tell you to start with. However, I have eliminated the concept of outlining for a story plot. Why? Because the plot tells us what to include in the story, but not why a reader would want to read it. Instead of plot, we will discuss the third element on our list of five elements, the story goal.

Taking this approach will enable you to see not only the topical requirements of these elements in your story but also the motivation necessary when crafting them. In a sense, **looking at it this way allows you to appeal to readers rather than just share your thoughts with them.** The same concept goes for the other elements. They need to be more personal and relatable rather than just presented on the page. You need to understand not just what they are but also understand them in a personal and meaningful way.

Let's look at the five elements from a motivational viewpoint:

1. Character - A hero we care about

   Often referred to as the "protagonist," your hero is so much more. He is a human being with habits, desires, fears, quirks, weaknesses, strengths, etc. All the things that make us identify with him and, therefore, care about him. Creating a truly dimensional character provides the backbone of your story. If readers don't care about your character or don't like or identify with him in any way, then they won't care about any of the story. In fact, the story goal or other characters, the epic battles, or the falling in love—none of this will matter if readers don't care about your hero.

2. Story Goal – Something we want

   What does your hero want? This is referred to as the story goal. The story goal is what the hero ultimately wants to happen in the end. Perhaps what he wants to change or gain, or, in many cases, to take back. It is the driving force behind everything he does, and it's what the reader expects to happen at the end. Achieving the story goal is what completes the heroic quest. The reader will identify with your hero and willingly take the journey right along with him. It is important to fully develop this area so that the reader wants it as much as the hero does.

3. Setting - The world we live in

   Setting is far too often minimized as primarily the location and time of your story. This is only a fraction of the value of this element because setting really encompasses the entire storyworld. Setting informs the characters and their lives, their culture, including how people dress and speak, their history, and what motivates them. The storyworld deserves attention and planning because it touches every single aspect of your story; it is present on every page and in every situation.

4. Conflict – The ways we suffer

   Conflict is a part of every story because it is a part of life. Without conflict, there is no value in achieving your story goal. In fact, many conflicts should get increasingly bigger. Conflict causes suffering. The hero must suffer, and, in kind, the reader will suffer right along with him. Suffering is a part of life and one that every human can identify with. Why? Because there must be a cost to attaining the story goal. Suffering helps us to value the achievement that much more. Just as some fitness gurus preach, "No pain, no gain."

5. Theme – The lesson we learn

   The lesson that the hero learns, and that in many cases is learned by all the primary characters, may seem trivial or unimportant when weighed against the other elements. In most cases, it is treated as a formulaic sub-plot. But what give a story substance are the lessons that are learned. In the absence of a moral arc, your story will be mere fluff and will not strike a chord deep inside the reader because, at our core, we are all born with an innate sense of right and wrong. We expect every story to recognize that human condition and share in the journey we travel to learn those lessons.

Now that you understand the five elements a bit more let's explore each one as we dig deeper into our premise and develop more of our story outline.

Character

To write a truly great story, one that people are willing to buy and read, it all starts with the hero. You can have an amazing storyline filled with action, adventure, villains, and epic battles, but if the main character is flat, too cliché, or even unlikeable, you will turn the reader off. The battle is meaningless when readers don't care if the hero wins or not. If they dislike the hero because, well, he's just a punk, then they will probably be fine if he dies in the end. It's also possible, and I've felt this way when reading some books that shall remain nameless, that if the "hero" is a real jerk, the reader might want to kill him themselves. Not good.

Most likely, if the hero is flat or a cliché, readers won't even bother reading through to the climactic moment. Most likely, they have already moved on to another story. They have better things to do with their time. I want you to be aware of that.

First off, let's remember what makes up the character element:

Character - A hero we care about

Often referred to as the "protagonist," your hero is so much more. He is a human being with habits, desires, fears, quirks, weaknesses, strengths, etc. All the things that make us identify with him and, therefore, care about him. Creating a truly dimensional character provides the backbone of your story. If readers don't care about your character or don't like or identify with him in any way, then they won't care about any of the story. In fact, the story goal or other characters, the epic battles, or the falling in love—none of this will matter if readers don't care about your hero.

People care about people they know, people they identify with, or people they sympathize with. Think about the people in your family and your friends. Then think about the people at the restaurant where you had dinner or who you sat next to in the library. The reality is that you don't care about their lives because you don't know them. Bad things happen to people all the time. Just watch the news for about a minute. Unfortunately, other people's tragedies do not really affect us. We don't *know* those people.

It is vital for your reader to identify with your main character. That is difficult to achieve in a short story, so you must be very intentional about how you create them. How is this done? By helping them to become a "real" person.

The general statistics of a person, i.e., height, weight, interests, or hobbies, don't necessarily tell us much about them. **We don't identify with people because they look or act like us. Rather, we identify with their human qualities, their flaws, fears, and desires.** We will use you as an example to begin.

I want to know about the things that really make you who you are. If I know nothing about what really matters most to you or how things make you feel, and all I have is your personal resume, I won't identify with you. For example, if I know your name and physical characteristics as well as your favorite hobbies etc., I still don't know you. Therefore, you are what is known as a "flat character." Flat characters lack the complexity that makes real-life people so fascinating.

To get to know you as a person, I need to ask more intentional questions. Some are deep, and some are specific. Answer the following questions about yourself:

> What is the best thing you can ever remember happening to you?

What do you dislike most about having (or not having) siblings?

Do you cry a lot? Why or why not?

What is your favorite food and why?

What do you fear most in life?

> What things would be on your bucket list and why?

Author Donald Maass writes that **what shapes us and gives our lives meaning is not the things that happen to us but their significance to us.** As we experience the events of our days, we process them and make them personal. We document our lives not just with visual images but also with narration that explains what those images mean. We are not just personal resumes or the dry sum of our accomplishments and failures. We are stories.

Your hero has a story that needs to be told. You need to know what makes him who he is. What events shaped his life? He must become a dimensional character who does more than act and react in expected ways. Every person is unique, and what he has been through or experienced, and his reactions to those will shape who he is and the choices he makes in your story.

It is still important to get a complete visual of him, including his basic details, so that you can "see" him in your story, just don't be afraid to delve into the complex personality that will be necessary to make your hero be believable and someone that we care about.

It is time to start fleshing out your character in ways that will give him dimension. All great characters start with one thing, and that is a name.

You must select names that will fit your story. Historical stories utilize classic names, often biblical ones, and fantasy stories have characters with names that are very unusual. Different countries also have names specific to their culture. It is a good idea to Google popular names from your country or time era before you begin.

From this list of names, select one to be your hero and perhaps use some others for supporting characters. You may wait to choose a name until you complete the character sketch. Either way, the name will be significant, and it will be personal to you.

> Write down all the potential names for your character here:

A character sketch is an integral part of making turning your character into a real person. You need to know your fictional character inside and -out before you can ever write a realistic, complicated, dimensional character that readers will care about. The best way to do that is to make sure your character is near your own age and gender. While not a requirement, it will be very difficult for you to write a realistic character when you are not familiar with all the nuances that make a person inherently male or female. The thought patterns and speech of an adult are vastly different from that of a teen. To write a character that you will truly know, it is best to start with one that you actually do know; one like yourself.

It is crucial that you take this next step very seriously. Don't skim through it with an "I don't know" attitude because by the time you sit down to write your story, you will have a flat character, and there is little you can do to change it at that point.

Use your imagination to see your character as a real person. You can be inspired by the traits and features of people you know or public figures. The more you put into this character sketch, the easier it will be to write your story, as you will understand everything the hero feels and does because you truly do know your hero inside and out. Some of these details might seem insignificant, and most of them will never be written into the story itself, but this exercise helps you get to see your main character as a real person.

CHARACTER SKETCH - THE HERO

Character's Full Name: _____

Gender: _____

Nickname (if any):

Reason or Story Behind Nickname:

Appearance-

Age: _____

Eye Color: _____

Hair Color: _____

Glasses or Contacts: _____

Weight: _____

Height: _____

Body Type/Build: _____

Skin Tone: _____

Shape of Face: _____

Distinguishing Marks/Scars: _____

Predominant Feature: _____

Healthy or has Disability or Ailment: _____

How does Character Dress:

Jewelry or Other Accessories:

Most Prized Possession: (Why?)

Favorites -

Favorite Color and Why:

Least Favorite Color and Why:

Favorite Music and Why:

Least Favorite Music and Why:

Favorite Foods:

Least Favorite Foods:

Favorite Literature:

Favorite Activities or Hobby:

Personality - (be detailed!)

Loud or Quiet (give examples):

Daredevil or Cautious (give examples):

What (event or person) made him that way:

Morals (Positive Ideals):

Motivation for Morals:

Optimist or Pessimist (give examples):

Introvert or Extrovert (give examples):

Good/Positive Characteristics (not physical):

Character Flaws:

Skills:

Minor Accomplishments:

Skills:

Darkest Secret:

Does anyone know the secret?:

How do they know?:

Habits -

Good Habits:

Bad Habits:

How do they relax or unwind?:

Physical habits with their body: (twitches, cracking knuckles, tossing hair)

Speaking Habits: (common used words/phrases)

Do they have to control any habits? Why and How?:

Background -

Where Born:

Type of Childhood:

Early Memories:

Significant Childhood Event(s):

Why or Why not does it still affect them?:

Education (what level and where or by whom):

Religion:

Finances:

Do they have a job? (Give details):

Family - (be detailed)

Mother's Name:

Relationship with Mother: (good or bad)

Why is the relationship this way:

Father's Name:

Relationship with Father:

Why is the relationship this way:

Siblings: (names and ages)

Explain the relationship with each sibling:

Extended family members:

Are they close?: (Why or why not)

Adopted family:

Are they close?: (Why or why not)

Attitude - (give examples)

Most at ease when:

Uncomfortable when:

Life Priorities (what matters most to them):

Past Failures or Embarrassments:

If granted one wish, what would it be?:

Why:

Self-Perception -

One word they would use to describe themselves:

One paragraph they would use to describe themselves:

What do they consider their best physical characteristic:

What is their worst:

Are they realistic assessments:

If not, why:

What 4 things character would most like to change about himself & why:

1.

2.

3.

4.

Relationship to Others -

How does character get along with...

Strangers:

Friends:

How are they perceived by...

Strangers:

Friends:

What impression does character give to most people:

Is this on purpose: (why or why not)

What do family/friends like most about character:

What do family/friends like least about character:

Who are character's best friend(s) and how do they know each other:

Person character was most influenced by: (Why?)

Person that character secretly admires: (Why?)

Problems and Crisis -

How does character react...

In a crisis:

When faced with problems:

To change:

How will any of these change the character?:

The Others

The world is full of people. Almost eight billion people, in fact. Your storyworld is also full of people; it might even be full of animals, fantastic creatures, or aliens. Typically, however, it's full of people. These are your secondary characters, aka…The Others. Unfortunately, too many of these other characters are just not believable. They enter and exit the story with little thought from the reader. They are, in fact, forgettable.

The value of your cast of supporting characters to the story is vastly underestimated. Their ability to give deeper insight and dimension to the hero's journey should be given due attention. They do not have to be forgettable. They can engage the reader as strongly as the hero does.

As an author, you need to find ways to make them multi-dimensional, conflicted, or even surprising. Give them a personality and problems. Make them challenge not only themselves but also those around them. Especially the hero.

Here is a list of typical supporting characters in an adventure story: the villain, the mentor, the sidekick, the love interest, the family, and the gang. The villain is your antagonist, and you must have some force working against your hero. This may or may not be the hero vs. a villain; there are other options for the main conflict. We will cover those in more detail later in this chapter when we discuss conflict.

Not all characters will be developed in this manner. You will have peripheral characters. Those that play a brief role, like a waitress or police officer. You do not need to give their name or many details. Simply refer to them by their role like, "the officer." Sometimes, an author will use a physical trait in place of a name for a peripheral character. This can be a moniker like, "blond dude" or "creepy old guy." For example:

> *I sat down on the bench next to this old man wearing a beige weathered jacket, a stained pair of pants three sizes too big, and white socks peeking out above those old guy shoes; the ones with two-inch soles that were made of rubber. His sullen look was probably etched into his face permanently by years of frowning. He looked like he could torture small animals and bratty children with one look from his rheumy eyes. Creepy old guy glanced at me briefly before returning to glare at the pigeons that had come begging for crumbs that would never come.*

These characters are used to interact with the main characters only briefly. They either help build the setting or advance the story in some way. These peripheral characters do not need to be developed here. You will write them into your story in a limited capacity.

If you choose to introduce additional characters that will have a supporting role, I have supplied some character worksheets for you to fill out. These characters may not be as in-depth as your hero, but they must also be developed as "real" people.

CHARACTER WORKSHEET

Character Name _____

Sketch or Paste Image

NickName _____

Physical Description

POSITIVE IDEALS

Personality

NEGATIVE IDEALS

Habits / Quirks

Goals and Motivations

Background

CHARACTER WORKSHEET

Character Name _____

Sketch or Paste Image

NickName _____

Physical Description
_____

POSITIVE IDEALS

Personality
_____
_____
_____

NEGATIVE IDEALS

Habits / Quirks
_____
_____

Goals and Motivations

Background
_____
_____
_____

CHARACTER WORKSHEET

Character Name _____

Sketch or Paste Image

NickName _____

Physical Description

POSITIVE IDEALS

Personality

NEGATIVE IDEALS

Habits / Quirks

Goals and Motivations

Background

CHARACTER WORKSHEET

Character Name _____

Sketch or Paste Image

NickName _____

Physical Description

POSITIVE IDEALS

Personality

NEGATIVE IDEALS

Habits / Quirks

Goals and Motivations

Background

Story Goal

The story goal is the driving force behind the plot of your story. It's what the hero wants or needs to obtain. In *Lord of the Rings,* the story goal was to destroy the ring. In *Star Wars IV A New Hope*, it was to destroy the Death Star. The hero is working toward one end, to achieve the story goal, and that is the fuel to the engine that drives him forward. We referenced this earlier as the plot.

It may seem logical to you that to write a truly epic story, you have to have a complicated plot with intricate goals and hidden agendas. However, the most memorable story goals are ones that can be summed up in one moment and one picture. In *Lord of the Rings,* everyone wanted to see Frodo drop the ring into the fire of Mount Doom, and in *Star Wars*, we just wanted the Death Star to blow up. When that happened, we knew the story was essentially over, and we could rest from all the tension that had been built up to that point. We got what we wanted.

With a short story, although your plot will be simpler than a long novel, it will still be a matter of establishing a specific story goal for your hero to attain.

Let's review what the story goal is:

> Story Goal - Something we want
>
> The story goal is what the hero ultimately wants to happen in the end. Perhaps what he wants to change or gain, or in many cases, to take back. It is the driving force behind everything he does, and it's what the reader expects to happen at the end. Achieving the story goal is what completes the heroic quest. The reader will identify with your hero and willingly take the journey right along with him; it is important to fully develop this area so that the reader wants it as much as the hero does.

The story goal is not necessarily your hero's initial desire or motivation. In some cases, your hero must go against what he wants in the beginning to reach the story goal. Frodo wanted to protect those he loved, so he chose to take the journey to destroy the ring. What he really desired was to be left alone in the Shire. The contrast between what the hero desires for himself and the story goal can make for a compelling contrast and opportunity for personal suffering. The hero will obviously accept the challenge and save the world, but it doesn't mean he started out with that mindset.

Remember that the goal of all stories is to create an emotional experience. To plan out a story goal that your reader cares about, **you need to understand the story goal in terms of need and want.** Your character will pursue the story goal based on both external goals and internal needs. The external goal is the resting place of the plot. In Frodo's case, the story goal was to destroy the ring. The internal needs are what create the emotional experience. Frodo wanted and needed to save his friends and loved ones.

Answer the following questions:

> What does your character want to happen at the end?

> Why does he want that?

> What are the obstacles to him achieving that goal?

Donald Maass writes brilliantly about story goal (plot) in terms of something we want:

> We all yearn. Things happen to us. We cope, solve problems, suffer setbacks, get somewhere, and pursue our dreams. What, though, actually drives us to do those things? It is something inside that has little to do with our challenges and goals. It's a need to relieve inner anxiety, prove something, love and be loved, rage at what's unfair, fit in, stand out, or find what will make us happy. It is important to understand that the inner and outer journeys work together to create an emotional journey

Just remember, internal motivation is the fuel the hero will run on. Maybe your hero will save the refugees because he wants to avenge the death of his friends, or perhaps he will fight in the civil war as a spy because he desires freedom for all slaves?

External motivation will be those things that are thrust upon your hero. He might be a merchant ship's crewman during wartime when the crew is attacked and shipwrecked on a beach in enemy territory. He must survive the natural elements, like weather and hunger, and the continued threat from his enemy, all while trying to get home. Your story goal is an intertwined relationship between what needs to happen and why the hero is willing to do it.

> Write your story goal here:

Setting

The setting informs everything else in the story. For example, in *The Chronicles of Narnia* by C.S. Lewis, Narnia would have been a completely different story if Lewis had written that the wardrobe dumped the Pevensie children on a tropical island instead of a snowy forest. The setting of Narnia influenced the characters and actions. The ice and snow lent to the characterization of the White Witch, and the journey would have been so different if Narnia itself was not the magical kingdom that Lewis created.

Let's revisit what setting is from the previous section...

> Setting - The world we live in
>
> Setting is far too often minimized as primarily the location and time of your story. This is only a fraction of the value of this element because setting really encompasses the entire storyworld. Setting informs the characters and their lives, their culture, including how people dress and speak, their history, and what motivates them. The storyworld deserves attention and planning because it touches every single aspect of your story; it is present on every page and in every situation.

The storyworld is more than just a static backdrop for your story; it is a dynamic aspect of storytelling. How you build and relate your storyworld will have a direct effect on your reader's emotional involvement. The setting is a moving, changing, and exciting part of your story.

Building your story's physical and cultural world is vital to convince your reader that your story is "real." Setting should be a part of every aspect of your story. It's not only in the description (detail mode) but also in the summary and dialogue. What sort of world does your hero inhabit? Is it a fantasy with mythical creatures and gravity-defying citizens, or historic America with its plantations and factories? All these will have their own geography, landscape, weather, architecture, temperature, and language.

The setting will help create emotion by showing the readers what you want them to feel in a certain scene. A great example is Earnest Cline's *Ready Player One*. The setting is a gloomy 2045, and the late James Halliday's parallel virtual universe, metaphorically called the "Oasis," removes the burden of a depressing daily life for its millions of online users who prefer the vast and colorful cyber world over their own dismal reality. The young hero, Wade Watts, comes from such a distressing situation that Cline describes in such stark terms, that readers cannot help but feel bleak about life in 2045. The setting does more than just usher the reader into a dystopian future; it sets the standard for how every character action is motivated by desperation or resignation.

We experience life as feelings. We go through events in our lives, but those would be nothing without the accompanying emotions. Like feeling the fear of jumping off a cliff to water forty feet below or the peace of sipping lemonade in the shade on a warm summer day. **The character's setting may not be as important as how he reacts to that setting.** If it's hot and everyone is dehydrated, sweating profusely, and wretched, how do the characters *react* to those conditions? That is the approach your setting should be taking; **not just the world around them, but how the inhabitants feel and interact within that world.**

For example, I love cold weather. Anything below 50 degrees is my happy place. I'm not sure why; it just is that way. My husband prefers suffocating warmth. Ugh! A few years ago, we were caught in a freak snowstorm. Several feet of snow had dropped overnight and during the day, the temperature hovered around five degrees. For me, I was thrilled because I had my heavy jacket, boots, and gloves. I played in the snow for hours!

My husband was absolutely miserable. His teeth chattered, and his lips turned a deep shade of purple when he went outside to clear snow from the stairs. At those temperatures, he wants to stay indoors and would almost rather starve than go out in the freezing snow. He's missing out, in my opinion, but you see that creating a setting is not as important as the added dimension that comes from the character's interaction with that setting. If I were a character and you put me in the snow, it would be a winter wonderland. If my husband were a character and you put him in the snow, it would be an impending disaster. Same setting, different experiences.

Before you start brainstorming every detail about your storyworld, just remember that creating the setting can be as much in what you show your readers as what you don't show them. When I was a kid, we used to watch an old television show called the Twilight Zone. It was the great "suspense" show of our generation and only came in black and white. You would think that would lack the ability to really set the scene. Not so. I remember one episode that stood out from so many others in my memory. The scene opens in what appears to be an average Midwestern town. There are homes, cars, businesses, and billboards. What I quickly noticed about this little slice of Americana was that there were no children. None! Lots of "normal" adults going about their idyllic lives, but not a single child in the entire town. The absence of children in a traditional small town set a more dramatic story plot twist than anything else could.

How many settings you have in a short story is up to you and the story you are telling. Use the below research worksheets to map out an overview of your storyworld. I have provided plenty of worksheets so you can have more than one location. This is a general brainstorm, and you can come back and make changes as your story develops.

Conflict

I remember watching television shows when I was growing up. We did not have on-demand services like Netflix, Amazon, or Hulu. Back then, there was no such thing as the Internet or even movie rentals. There were no electronic devices to play movies on. Outside of theaters or drive-ins, television was all we had, and even that was limited.

One show that my dad loved, and by proxy I watched, was *Star Trek*. Those of you Chris Pine fans are nodding your heads in recognition. However, in the "old days" of *Star Trek*, William Shatner played the heroic Captain James T. Kirk. It was immensely popular, and millions tuned in every week to watch the Starship Enterprise's adventures in space exploration.

One of the most recognizable things from that show was the captain's chair. It was not a marvel of design and had no special powers, but it's where he sat for 79 episodes. It was iconic.

Paramount Pictures sold Captain Kirk's chair in 2002, and a Trekkie fan picked it up for a mere $304,750! That's about the price of a modest home in most cities; at a minimum, it's enough to buy a high-end Ferrari. Regardless of what any of us would have done ourselves, that chair did not seem worth the price that was paid for it.

Was Captain Kirk's chair worth almost $305,000 dollars? Most people would say, "No, it wasn't."

You would be wrong. The truth is that the chair was worth that much.

Why? Because someone was willing to pay that much for it.

One of the most elemental rules of a capitalist society is that a thing's value, or worth, is the equivalent of the highest amount someone is willing to pay for it. This is why the cost of attaining a story goal is so critical to storytelling. **The true value of a story goal is best**

determined by what your hero is willing to suffer, or "pay," to attain it. Frodo suffered deeply throughout the entire trilogy just to destroy the evil ring of power in the fires of Mt. Doom.

Let's review what the element of conflict is:

> Conflict - The ways we suffer
>
> Conflict is a part of every story because it is a part of life. Without conflict, there is no value in achieving your story goal. In fact, many conflicts should get increasingly bigger. Conflict causes suffering. The hero must suffer, and, in kind, the reader will suffer right along with him. Suffering is a part of life and one that every human can identify with. Why? Because there must be a cost to attaining the story goal. Suffering helps us to value the achievement that much more. Just as some fitness gurus preach, "No pain, no gain."

Suffering is the key to establishing value, and therefore, just allowing your hero to get shot or break a limb will not cut it. You will have to reach deeper levels for there to be true suffering, even to the point that your readers will suffer with your hero. That is vital so they can rejoice when the hero attains the story goal.

Conflict should build and increase throughout your story. You must keep raising the stakes for your hero. This will take planning. Watch for downtime. If your hero is happy and healthy, chances are there is no conflict. Unless this is the calm before the coming storm, avoid too many quiet and content scenes. In this section, you will brainstorm some possible conflicts that your hero might face.

Let's briefly look at the different types of conflict. The following table will show you the main types of conflict in stories.

Person v. Person	Person v. Self	Person v. Society
In this type of conflict, a character clashes with another character. It can also be an animal or other living being.	This is typically a dilemma; doubt, lack of confidence, or a touch choice. Although the conflict is within the character, it most likely affects others.	This is more common than you might think. A character challenges a law, institution, culture, or tradition. He battles against those that represent these things.
Person v. Nature	**Person v. Technology**	**Person v. Supernatural**
The character is fighting to overcome forces of nature. This could be survival, navigating, or meeting basic needs.	The character is resisting or fighting technological forces. Either a super computer taking over the world or resistance to using certain technology at all.	The character is battling any force that is not of this world. Whether monsters or aliens, some otherworldly force that may have powers will take on the hero to total domination.

Many authors will have more than one type of conflict in their story, but only if it makes sense. A story about the hardships of the Oregon Trail or a medieval dictator will not have person v. technology and, generally, not person v. supernatural. These will have strong person v. nature and person v. self or society conflict.

In a short story, multiple types of conflict are difficult to represent fully. It is best if you choose one mode of conflict and let that be the basis of your antagonist (or antagonistic force). If you are particularly drawn to two conflicts, make sure they go well together, like person v. self and person v. nature. In this case, your hero has many internal issues and a character arc while externally battling deadly nature. Now, let's discuss external and internal suffering.

External Suffering:

Just as conflicts and challenges will build to a climactic point, so should your hero's suffering. If there is too much too soon, readers will react to the constant stimulation only to be disappointed by the anticlimactic nature of the final scene. In essence, the worst is over, and it all seems boring by comparison.

Most of what the hero will suffer will be a result of his own choices. For example, he suffers because he made a decision that should bring him closer to the story goal, but it came with severe consequences, he is stabbed in the leg because he fights to protect the village, or his father is killed because he refuses to betray the rebels to the evil king.

Everything has a price, and suffering is the price to be paid in every hero's story. The suffering must make sense. Random suffering will not establish a value because it will confuse the plot and bewilder the reader. As the hero takes more aggressive action to attain the story goal, and as his actions become bigger and bolder, so must the suffering and subsequent setbacks.

External suffering is essentially physical suffering. It might not be as emotionally moving as internal suffering, but it is a consequence of taking risks and fighting the bad guy. It is important not to overdo physical suffering as it may minimize or even turn the reader off. No one likes to read about torture, so it's best not to prolong it. Limit the amounts and perhaps be willing to imply the physical pain rather than state it.

Physical suffering is not always a result of an injury, either. It does not have to have your hero laid up in the medic station with round-the-clock nursing care. It can be a stomach virus after the villain poisons the hero's soup or even flu during a winter storm when the hero and his gang are trying to cross a mountain pass to escape the villain's army.

Physical pain can take many forms. Something does not have to be cut off, and blood does not even have to be involved for there to be physical pain. Physical suffering can be an inconvenience or discomfort. The best idea is to make the suffering match the scene and always make sure it is rising action and rising conflict.

Fill out the following worksheets to brainstorm physical suffering.

EXTERNAL SUFFERING

EVENT	SUFFERING

EVENT	SUFFERING

EVENT	SUFFERING

EXTERNAL SUFFERING

EVENT	SUFFERING
EVENT	SUFFERING
EVENT	SUFFERING

Internal Suffering:

Internal suffering is emotional suffering, and it traps the reader on a roller coaster of emotions. They may not like what is happening to the character, but it will draw them into the story. **Internal suffering will have a far greater impact on your reader than physical suffering.** Since the story goal will compel the hero to keep moving forward, it is reasonable to assume they will make devastating mistakes along the way.

For emotional suffering to affect the reader, we need to explore the concept of emotions from the "showing" vs. "telling" modes of writing. The most common mistake by new authors is that they tell the reader about all the emotions the hero is having and then expect the reader to automatically feel the same thing. Let me give you an example:

> *I walked into the darkened alley and felt an overwhelming fear come over me. I could barely breathe as my eyes darted in every direction, looking for danger to materialize from the black depths. I knew he was here somewhere. My heart was pounding a mile a minute, and I felt like I was going to faint. I had my hands out in front of me, trying to find my way. It was so black that I could not see any obstacles in my path. I felt like a blind person and struggled to take each step. My breathing was so loud I was sure the entire city of Cleveland could hear the puffing. I wanted to run away, but I knew I had to conquer my fear and move forward.*

That was definitely a scary situation. So, were you scared? Maybe you at least felt tension? To be honest, you probably didn't feel anything. Maybe you are like me and were too busy rolling your eyes. Why? Because, I was spoon-feeding you emotions that you probably don't feel. Okay, it's a dark alley, and a crazed murderer is on the loose. So what? What if you are curled up with a blanket on your couch at home with a fire in the fireplace? You're probably not nervous; you're bored.

As an author, it is your job to provoke natural feelings in your readers, not dish them on a platter of tasteless clichés. Let's try this again:

> *The alley wasn't just dark, it was pure black. I had never seen such a complete absence of color. The massive buildings that sandwiched this narrow strip of asphalt were hidden in plain sight. It was just me and two hundred thousand tons of chipped concrete and broken glass. Not even the moonlight dared to enter this unholy place. Far behind me, the lights of the downtown Cleveland theater district glittered brightly, but even that was not enough to help me. They knew better than to shine here. No one wanted to know what went on in this alley. I told myself that maybe this was all just an optical illusion and that no one was there. No one was stalking me. Taking a deep breath, I forced myself forward, trembling hands outstretched into the void. I couldn't hear any sound aside from my own shallow breathing. I told myself that I was alone, but I knew better. I knew he was somewhere nearby, waiting. I knew he could hear me.*

Were you scared? Or a little nervous, at least? In the second version of this scene I did not give you even one detail with internal emotion. Any suffering or fear was implied by the situation. Look at the key showing words like "unholy," "absence," and "void." Stating that he could hear her breathing has a greater effect at creating tension than a clichéd scene where a knife-wielding murderer is hiding behind a dumpster waiting to jump. Choosing words and statements that convey the situation itself will more often affect your reader's emotional response than telling a character's reactions to the situation.

This woman was in the alley, and she knew she was in danger. Her fear was evident by the words I chose in the description. I showed you the situation, but I did not tell you her feelings or any reactions she was experiencing. I simply presented a fearful situation and allowed you to respond to it. We will go into greater detail about showing vs. telling in Chapter Five with the three modes of fiction.

Here are some types of emotional suffering:

   Humiliation, guilt, loss, fear, loneliness, rejection, betrayal, injustice, and embarrassment.

Any one of these will elicit more sympathy for your hero than a broken leg. These will go straight to the heart and pull those strings. Why? Because every person has most likely endured many or all of these emotions at some point in their life. Readers will relate to the suffering and, therefore, they will feel it.

Although physical pain will affect the readers' thoughts and opinions, it is not necessarily an emotional experience for them. Essentially, there is little we can relate to unless we have also been shot, sliced, had broken ribs, or experienced any other form of physical suffering your hero will endure. It's not to say it will have no effect; it's just less likely that we can relate.

Emotional pain goes right for the jugular. It's deep and excruciating. **When readers identify with or have feelings for your hero, they will experience that internal pain and suffer along with your hero.** Remember that the value of the story goal is based on how much your hero is willing to pay for it. Emotional suffering is a big price tag and will make the attainment of the story goal that much more satisfying for the reader.

As you did in the previous exercise, you will brainstorm possible suffering that your hero may endure. Fill out the following worksheets to brainstorm some emotional suffering your character might experience. You will want to come back to this section after you have completed your outline in Chapter Four and made revisions. But for now, just get some thoughts down.

INTERNAL SUFFERING

EVENT		SUFFERING
EVENT	»	SUFFERING
EVENT		SUFFERING

INTERNAL SUFFERING

EVENT	SUFFERING

EVENT	SUFFERING

EVENT	SUFFERING

Theme

Stories must have a moral structure. Without that structure, it is not a story but rather a series of events. There must be good vs. evil for conflict and resolution to occur. It is the concept of a moral structure that will be the foundation of the hero's lesson.

The lesson your hero will learn is referred to as the story's theme. It is basically a short phrase that establishes a specific statement about a moral truth. The theme is often woven into the character arc and supported by every other element of your story. The storyworld, characters, and conflict will all contribute to the hero learning a lesson.

Let's review what the theme is:

> Theme - The lesson we learn
>
> The lesson that the hero learns, and that in many cases is learned by all the primary characters, may seem trivial or unimportant when weighed against the other elements. In most cases, it is treated as a formulaic sub-plot. But what give a story substance are the lessons that are learned. In the absence of a moral arc, your story will be mere fluff and will not strike a chord deep inside the reader because, at our core, we are all born with an innate sense of right and wrong. We expect every story to recognize that human condition and share in the journey we travel to learn those lessons.

The theme will connect all the parts of your story. Readers will not consciously know that it is there, but deep down, they will expect it. Without a theme, they will feel somewhat lost and probably let down at the end of the story. To them, your story will lack purpose, and as human beings, we all need purpose. Purpose involves change and understanding.

For example, in the best-selling novels turned blockbuster movie series, *Jurassic Park,* author Michael Crichton shows the calamity that comes from human greed, complacency, and scientific knowledge unrestrained by ethics, morality, and basic wisdom. John Hammond started as a man excited by possibility but fueled by greed. In the end, he saw the repercussions of his actions and finally agreed that the natural order of life is best left to itself.

At no point in the book or the movie did anyone tell you what the theme was. It was evident in the characters, plot, conflict, and story goal. A theme does not need to be profound, and most are not. There is nothing new under the sun. **The theme needs simply to appeal to our human emotions and intellect.** It needs to be the lesson we learn.

To get a general sense of the lesson that will matter to you, start by writing down moral or personal issues that you are passionate about. They can be personal struggles or moral compromises you see in our society or in others around you. Regardless of how you think it will fit with your story, make a list of every single one of them and why they are important to you.

> **Moral or social issues I am passionate about:**

As part of the lesson, let's talk about ideals and the character arc. An ideal is a goal or trait that signifies some greater meaning. It's what the character believes in and what motivates him. Ideals matter substantially to your story, and they inform the actions of your characters. A character arc is the transformation or inner journey of a character over the course of a story. Some would even say Character Arc = Theme.

Ideals can be either positive or negative. Remember, they signify greater meaning, and that can be good or bad. Here are some examples:

Positive ideals: Life, beauty, love, charity, forgiveness, protection, and humility.

Negative Ideals: Selfishness, Destruction, Disdain, Resentment, Hate, Pride, Revenge

> **List more positive and negative ideals here:**

As mentioned before, ideals inform your characters' actions, but they also define the conflict between them. Conflict occurs when a positive and a negative ideal collide. One will overcome the other, and that is the contributing factor to the theme of your story.

Your hero should embody a positive ideal like love, honesty, courage, wisdom, etc. Most heroes also have a negative ideal. Nobody is perfect, after all. Remember, a character needs to be relatable. Some might even have a lot of negative ideals. Most of us know about Scrooge in A Christmas Carol. A negative ideal is commonly referred to as a character flaw. Everyone has a character flaw of some kind; however, negative ideals should never outweigh positive ones in your hero for him to attain the story goal.

In some circumstances, the negative outweighs the positive in the beginning, and this is the foundation for your character arc. Your hero can start out with a negative ideal(s) and through circumstances and plot twists, end with a positive ideal. Change happens. Think about Han Solo in *Star Wars Episode IV*. He started out as a selfish, unreliable gambler who only cared about what would benefit him. That is dramatically different from the Han Solo we know in later episodes. He became a hero who would sacrifice his life for those of his friends.

Below are some classic examples of famous character arcs:

Emma by Jane Austin

Character - Emma

Start - Determinedly single, interferes in others' lives, a bit of a snob

Finish - Humbled by love and repentant for matchmaking attempts that caused harm to others

It's a Wonderful Life by Philip Van Doren Stern, originally a short story titled The Greatest Gift

Character - George Bailey

Start - Restless in a small town, wants more out of life, thinks there is bigger and better out there

Finish - Realizes the importance of accomplishments; friends and family are the most important thing.

A character's change does not always mean moving from bad (negative) to good (positive) but can be from foolish (negative) to wise (positive) or ignorant (negative) to enlightened (positive).

Remember George Bailey from *It's a Wonderful Life*? He was likable from the very start. He's a good person and is loved and respected. His problem, his negative ideal, is that he is ignorant of his value and true circumstances. He believes that everyone would be better off without him, so he attempts suicide. A hapless angel named Clarence intervenes in a different way than one would think and grants George his wish; he was never born.

Through his experiences as a non-existent person, Henry sees the chain of events that result from his never having been born. He never saved his brother Harry from falling through the ice. He was never a pilot, so he did not save all the soldiers whose ship the Japanese attacked. The negative changes in the world around him show George his true value, even to the point of life and death. The character arc comes when George rejects the lie and is enlightened to his purpose in life. George did not go from bad to good but from ignorant to enlightened.

It is time for you to brainstorm some positive and negative ideals that may inspire your character arc and maybe inform your villain's behaviors and create conflict. Remember that ideals occur in every person, whether positive or negative, and they present themselves within oneself (internal conflict) or between two characters (external conflict).

These ideals will contribute to your lesson, story goal, and conflict (suffering). Brainstorm every potential ideal for your hero as well as your villain, if applicable. There is enough space in the chart for the ideals of the additional supporting cast, and you can come back later and fill these in after you complete your story outline in Chapter Four.

Fill out the Character Ideals Chart chart on the following page. You can use this for as many characters as you want, but it is essential for your primary characters.

Character	Positive Ideals	Negative Ideals

Remember, a character arc is the transformation or inner journey of a character over the course of a story, typically from negative to positive. When writing short stories, you will want a dimensional character that experiences an arc through the story, but you will not have time to go in-depth.

A hero's success and failure are often judged based on their actions. However, as an author, **it is your responsibility to understand that it is not so much the hero's actions as the motivation behind the actions that define the true success of attaining the story goal.** In *Divergent* by Veronica Roth, why did Tris Prior rebel against her chosen faction to save Abnegation lives? Orson Scott Card said, "A character is what he does, yes - but even more, a character is what he means to do." The story goal is what he wants, but the motivation that makes him want it is what forms the basis for the lesson he will learn, i.e., the theme.

Motivation comes not only from our values or personality but also from our fears and needs, our past, and those who have influenced us. This is where your character sketch will come in handy. It is well worth your time to go back and review your character so you can step into that role again and get in their mindset to truly understand what motivates them.

Pause, go back, and review your character sketch. Take your time. The more time you spend reviewing and envisioning your character from the inside out, the easier it will be to complete this next section. And most important, the more dimensional your character and his actions are, the more emotional the experience for the reader.

Remember, creating a moral, strong, skilled hero can bring excitement to your story. Use the Theme Mind Maps on the following pages to narrow down your ideas from this section and develop your hero's lesson. You have plenty of room to try more than one.

THEME MIND MAP

1. What negative ideal does the hero start with?

2. What motivated the hero to pursue the story goal?

The hero's lesson

3. What choices did the hero make that had devastating consequences?

5. How did the hero overcome and restore the negative consequences?

4. How did the negative consequences affect the hero and the story goal?

Notes:

Looking through the possible themes from your mind maps, select the one that you feel best reflects your own personal values. That can be done by selecting one or even combining more than one theme. Based on your selection, you will make a moral statement in which you feel strongly about its truth or validity. This is your hero's lesson.

> Write your hero's lesson here:

Now that you have explored the different elements of your story, revise and record some previously established information you will need to reference in later parts of this workbook:

> Write your story goal:

> Write the hero's lesson:

> Write your premise here:

CHAPTER FOUR

Getting Organized

A General Sketch

A general sketch of a story outlines the events in the broadest of terms. This is the point in the early planning that is exciting because you have a premise and a succinct summary of what your story will be about. At this point, your head is most likely spinning with ideas.

A successful general sketch is built on asking a lot of questions. Ask yourself the "whys" and "what ifs" of your premise, and then think about the results of those. These are what develop into your scenes. You can take the opportunity here to write every idea, no matter how random or off-beat it may seem. Believe it or not, many of these will appear as emotionally charged scenes in your story.

Don't worry too much about organization or linking these ideas in chronological order. The important part here is to just let the creative part of your brain pour itself onto the pages.

Before you begin, rewrite your premise here:

Now write everything you know about your story:

Go back over your general sketch and use one color to highlight every area that needs further fleshing out (brainstorming). Then, using a different color, highlight every idea that is solid. You can cross out any ideas that you are ready to dump outright. Make notes as necessary so that when you come back to review these scene notes, they will make sense. You can do this as you go through the next chapter; just come back and make notes, add, or subtract.

By this time, some of what you have worked out in your general sketch may have influenced your premise. If you want to make any adjustments to your premise, now is the time to make them. You may want to just tweak a few words but crafting your final premise will lead you solidly into the next chapter.

> Rewrite your premise here:

Congratulations! You have now transitioned from an "idea" to a working plan for your story. Let's move on and develop your story outline.

Your Outline

Unlike a novel in which you would outline each chapter, your short story outline will be an abbreviated sequence of events based on the five story elements and your general sketch. It is important to remember that this outline can change and evolve as you write your story. In fact, I am an avid outliner for everything I write. For this workbook, when writing the draft, I went back and revised my outline as I worked through the various chapters.

I have provided several outline worksheets for you. The first is a key elements planner and you can fill one out for the entire story or one for each major scene. The second is a key events timeline. You can write and revise several times as your story continues to evolve.

KEY ELEMENTS PLANNER

Goal
What does the hero want at the beginning of the story?

Conflict
What stops him from achieving his goal?

Disaster
What happens & how does the hero end up worse than before?

Reaction
What does the hero react emotionally? + or - ideals?

Dilemma
What possible options are available at the hero?

Decision
What does the hero decide to do? (what is his new path?)

KEY ELEMENTS PLANNER

Goal
What does the hero want at the beginning of the story?

Conflict
What stops him from achieving his goal?

Disaster
What happens & how does the hero end up worse than before?

Reaction
What does the hero react emotionally? + or - ideals?

Dilemma
What possible options are available at the hero?

Decision
What does the hero decide to do? (what is his new path?)

KEY EVENTS OUTLINE

Note the main events in this story.
Include general time event occurs (day/night, etc), duration (how long), location, and characters invloved.

▸
▸
▸
▸
▸
▸
▸
▸
▸
▸
▸

KEY EVENTS OUTLINE

Note the main events in this story.

Include general time event occurs (day/night, etc), duration (how long), location, and characters invloved.

-
-
-
-
-
-
-
-
-
-
-
-

KEY EVENTS OUTLINE

Note the main events in this story.
Include general time event occurs (day/night, etc), duration (how long), location, and characters invloved.

-
-
-
-
-
-
-
-
-
-
-
-

Starting Strong

A good short story starts off strong and quickly captures the reader. The opening is your only chance to hook your audience, and you don't want to lose your reader during the first paragraph. The beginning of a story sets the tone of the entire narrative and begins the setup towards the middle and ending. A good beginning will hook your reader and keep them turning pages to experience the world you've created.

Short stories have far less time to cover a lot of ground than novels do. **You must make the most of your opening few paragraphs.** Fortunately, there are many ways you can draw the reader in right from the start. Here are a few options to consider:

1. Hook readers with excitement. Start off with something that immediately engages the reader from the opening sentence, like an action scene or an unexpected event. The inciting incident is the moment your hero is pushed into the central conflict of your story, which can be an enticing scene to start with, and clues your viewers in on what kind of story this is going to be.

2. Introduce the lead character. Starting your short story by introducing your main character can be an effective way to draw the audience in emotionally, especially if this character is written in first-person, thereby establishing their worldview. Try giving your main character a unique voice or quirk that makes them interesting and intriguing to your readers. When readers care about someone, they want to know what's going to happen to them and will keep reading. Establish this feeling with your readers quickly within your short story to have an effective beginning.

3. Start with dialogue. A powerful line of dialogue from one of your characters as your first sentence can quickly establish who they are and what their point of view is. Readers will want to read on to discover who is saying this first line and what is going on. Here are some examples that would grab a reader's attention:

    "Get out of my personal space, you freak!"

    "Do you really think she is never coming home?"

    "Look at me carefully. Today is the last day you will ever see me alive."

    "No, don't!"

4. Begin with action or a mystery. Opening with action is what we mentioned above with the inciting incident. It is something that happens to propel your hero into action. You can open with an escape scene, something blowing up or crashing, or even a big argument. You can also present a mystery to your audience on the first page to create a compelling beginning that keeps them interested until it's solved. A mystery can also mean opening with a question or

an unsolvable problem, which will pique the curiosity of your reader, and they'll be excited to know what happens next. Either way you choose to go with this, make sure it is strong and relevant to the story goal and character.

Just remember, how you start will set the tone for the entire story. When you start strong and interesting, readers will be in the right frame of mind to eagerly read through to the end.

Scene Breaks

A scene break is just as it sounds; a break between two scenes within a chapter or a short story. Remember from Chapter One that a scene is a section of the overall story that contains its own unique combination of setting, character, dialogue, and sphere of activity. A scene break is a separation between related scenes. It's used to indicate time passing or a change of location that continues in the same scene.

A scene break is when you hit enter (or return) three times in a double-spaced document, leaving two blank lines between one section of text and the next section of text, or when you use asterisks, dotted lines, or a small graphic. In the following example, you can see how the scene break shows that time has passed:

> *Jessica was back at the computer that controlled the IV. Vincent looked up from the bed, their eyes met and everything else vanished—the lab and the humming machines and the lonely years since they had last been together—he was thankful she was here now. She closed her eyes and punched the key.*
>
> *The only thing Vincent could think of was the pain that would come. Would he even remember her when he woke up?*
>
> * * *
>
> *Vincent gasped for air and pulled at his restraints.*
>
> *He couldn't breathe. His chest was being crushed. He looked frantically towards the beeping machine.*
>
> *He expected Jessica to be at the computer station. He blinked for a moment to clear his sight. He did remember her! He scoured the room, looking for any sign of her, but the lab was empty.*

In this case, Vincent was unconscious for an unknown amount of time. It could have been minutes or hours, perhaps even days. It is unknown how long he was out, but it does not matter. Either way, an unknown amount of time elapsed.

This break was about keeping the tension and emotion flowing. In this scene, by evaporating the time away with a scene break, you keep the reader focused on the emotion.

This does not mean that you need to find ways to add scene breaks. Many short stories do not use them. You will know when it's necessary to the flow of events. Again, one of the best examples for you is to read a lot of short stories and pay attention to the formatting. Experience is often the best teacher.

Writing Mechanics | CHAPTER FIVE

The Illusion of Reality

What does fiction have to do with reality? After all, you may write an adventure story where a 15-year-old kid saves New York from an alien invasion. What is realistic about that? Nothing really. Readers don't want reality, but they do want the *illusion* of reality. It's a fine balance. There is something called the suspension of disbelief. This is defined as a willingness to suspend one's critical faculties and logic for the sake of enjoyment. Not only are they willing to believe, but they also want to.

Life, in general, is boring. If you think about how you spend your time, all twenty-four hours, seven days a week, what significant things happen in your life? Not many, probably. Well, not compared to finding lost treasure in a secret world or time travel. Would you want to read a play-by-play about your own life? Probably not. I know I would not want to read about mine.

I have several friends who are police officers who face life and death on the streets; they see things that would make our jaws hit the ground. One is on a gang task force; another is a K-9 officer who works with S.W.A.T. I have heard some of the craziest stories from my police friends. However, if they gave me "a day in the life of a police officer" it would consist of primarily patrolling the streets, writing reports, and coffee breaks. It would be boring! The exciting stuff (to us, at least) does not happen every day.

Every story we read needs to have rising action. However, to have an emotional response to it, we must also believe it's really happening. You would think that I could tell the story of my police friend by just cutting out the reports and uneventful patrols, but that is not correct either.

Good fiction is more than just reality minus the boring stuff. Good fiction is excitement and emotion in a constant movement towards a final goal. A goal that will provide closure and satisfaction. Fiction authors have incredible freedom to create an entire world in any way they want it to be. "In nonfiction writing, you're revealing a world; in fiction, you're constructing one," explains Penguin Random House copy editor Kathleen Go. "In this way, fiction readers look to you for that balance of fact and imagination." **There it is, young authors; a balance of fact and imagination.**

Now, knowing that does not necessarily mean you can write amazing super-charged scenes. Have you ever had such a tremendous experience and tried to tell a friend about it but found that you could not find the right words to express what it felt like? That is what the author faces; finding the right words to express the hero's failures, triumphs, and conflicts in a way that expresses the depth of emotion and yet retains a semblance of reality.

So how is it done? First, consider the five senses. Touch, taste, smell, sight, and hearing. To bring some reality to the fantastical world you will create, rely on the things that people relate to. The physical sensations of the world around them.

Next, be an observer. Everywhere you go, look, and listen to people. Consider how they walk, talk, interact, and behave in public. Observe your family at the dinner table. How does everyone talk to each other? Do they even sit around a dinner table? All too often, authors will write a scene to which the readers simply cannot relate. It's just not how people act or talk. Become a professional observer and write down your observations. They will come in handy.

> Observe any location with your senses and write a 350-word fictional narrative that is set in that location:

Three Modes of Fiction

Fiction has three primary types or modes of writing: summary, detail, and dialogue.

Summary mode is a way of imparting facts to the reader that are necessary to relay and move the story forward. This is also referred to as exposition. One purpose is to fill in the backstory or set the scene or character up. It's also used in transitions between scenes to get readers up to speed while time passes or if a new scene takes place in a different location from the previous scene. This is known as "telling."

Detail mode is primarily where you are describing a scene or person to the reader. Typically, this mode will elicit an emotional response in the reader. When you are showing the reader a part of the story, you are giving him the opportunity to see what you see and, thereby, step into your storyworld. This is referred to as "showing."

Here is a quick example of telling v. showing modes:

> Telling (summary): Antoine was terribly afraid of the dark.

> Showing (detail): His dad switched off the light and left the room. Antoine tensed and huddled further under the blankets. He gripped the sheets up to his neck and held his breath as he waited for his eyes to adjust to the abyss.

Dialogue mode is straightforward; it's when people talk to one another or even to themselves (inner dialogue). You can use dialogue to reveal a lot about your story or characters by what they say. Dialogue is a powerful tool when used correctly and realistically. Let's look at each mode in more detail.

Summary Mode:

The concept of the telling mode in story writing gets a bad rap. I've read all the author blogs about "Show, don't tell," and that is all well and good. We will get to that part in the next section. Telling, referred to as summary mode, is necessary to fill in vital information without losing your reader through paragraph after paragraph of descriptions about how long it takes to fly from San Francisco to Atlanta. It takes about five hours; just say it. There is no need to describe it. Say it and move on to the good stuff.

Here is a little secret that new authors really need to understand; too much detail can be boring! True story. Summary mode is most useful when you want to skip excessive details while still conveying information that is useful to that scene. Let's say, for instance, your character had to take that five-hour flight to Atlanta and get to an important board meeting where she would soon find out the vice president is trying to get her fired. You could write this:

> *She caught the red-eye out of San Francisco and landed in Atlanta at 5 a.m. the next morning.*

That is all it takes. We don't need the details of the flight, the long lines at the airport, or how exhausted she is but cannot sleep thanks to the fat sweaty guy snoring in the seat next to her (that really did happen to me on a flight). If she took a red-eye, she's tired, and the trip must be important. We get it.

This is not to say that you can't give any details at all in summary mode. You can disguise summary sentences with a few details to give interest, and you will still be in summary mode. For example:

> *She caught the red-eye out of San Francisco and landed in Atlanta while it was still dark. Crossing the near-empty terminal, she checked her watch for the third time. She had a few minutes to grab a Starbucks on her way downtown. Some liquid energy was just what she needed right now.*

Adding these details to the summary tells the reader a lot about her state of mind and the situation she is walking into. The issue can be deciding which facts are necessary and which are unnecessary. Don't stress too much about it. Even some seasoned authors slip into detail mode out of convenience or to show the readers how much research they have done. Too many facts and details will lose the reader, but not enough will not be compelling, so use summary mode to move things forward.

Last rule, extensive summary mode should never make its way onto the first page of your story. Outside of a few details, that is not the time to apply an information dump. An info dump is a large amount of information dumped into the reader's lap at one time. It is difficult to sift through and can be overwhelming.

Info dumps are a problem for many writers, especially new ones. Sometimes, it can be overzealous writing where the author just can't come up with an alternative way to convey the information that they think the reader has to know. Info dumps are an extended form of telling (rather than showing). These dumps are usually done through narration but can be found in dialogue as well.

Here is an example of an info dump in summary mode:

> *Melanie was her best friend. They were in the same fifth-grade class and spent every day together. On the day they met, they were at dance class at the downtown YMCA which was in a very old building. They both thought the class was kind of lame but had gone anyway. Melanie was the tallest girl in the class and stood right next to Jessica. The way her blond hair was curled and tied up in a high ponytail made her look almost like one of the teachers, rather than a student. Melanie had an openness about her that people responded to instantly. They laughed together about how goofy the boys looked dancing. There were no cute boys in that class and they both talked about how much more fun it would have been with some cute boys to dance with. Melanie was taller than the boys anyway, so there was not much hope of that happening. Melanie was obsessed with the color purple and always wore something purple. She especially loved wearing this one pair of purple tights with silver glitter stars. The teacher said she "sparkled" when she danced,*

but I was not sure if she meant the tights, or just that Melanie was a good dancer. After that, they started doing everything together.

Don't get caught up in giving too many details; most of them really don't matter. Just stick to what is necessary to build characters or setting.

> Write a fictional paragraph using summary mode:

Detail Mode:

Show don't tell. This is the mantra of many of those teaching the craft of writing to younger students. But as you learned in the previous section, it is only one narrative tool. That said, detail mode will encompass more text than the other two and is crucial to the success of the reader's experience.

You want your reader to not just see a scene but also to hear, touch, and feel what is happening. For that, you will be in detail mode. It is important to distinguish this from summary mode. You need to show your reader what is happening without actually telling them.

We touched on this in Chapter Three with emotional suffering. You cannot expect your reader to feel something simply because you tell them that your character feels it. In fact, write what a character feels, and quite the opposite will happen; the reader will probably not feel a thing. Most authors, unfortunately, have used sentences like, "She was so embarrassed her throat dried up," or, "When he heard the news, he felt like someone had punched him in the stomach." Write that, and it is pretty much guaranteed that readers will not feel any anxiety for the character.

Human beings are complex and have emotions at various levels, some on the surface that are evident and some running much deeper. As an author, you cannot expect to know how every reader will respond to any given situation. Therefore, to elicit true emotions, **you must create a scene in such a way as to provoke the reader's emotions naturally.**

Let's look at an example of telling the reader a character's emotions:

> *Drake stood silently and watched the scene unfolding across the street. A tall man in a dark hoodie stopped directly in front of the bar and pulled his hood lower, preventing Drake from seeing his face. Drake worried about what this guy was doing here so late at night. From his vantage point, he could see when the stranger turned around and stepped into the blue glow of the bar's CLOSED sign. The first thing he noticed was the dark, hooded eyes framed by a scar that ran from cheek to chin. He felt his heart drop. It was Jaeger! Drake's chest pounded. He thought he would never see that face again. He muttered a curse because he knew Jaeger was up to no good.*

Do you see what is happening in this paragraph? Practically every sentence is telling the reader what Drake is seeing, hearing, and feeling instead of just showing what he is seeing and hearing and letting the reader feel. Every time you write that a character saw, smelled, heard, or felt something, you need to reword the sentence to show the reader just what it is the character is seeing, smelling, etc. In most instances, the rewrite only requires a few word changes and perhaps a little maneuvering of phrases. The difference is often subtle, but it can produce powerful results. Here's a rewrite:

> *Drake tucked back into the shadows of the alley. Across the street, a tall man in a dark hoodie, pulled low to obscure his face, stopped directly in front of the bar. The neon CLOSED sign washed the sidewalk in pale blue, revealing broken bottles, cigarette butts, and discarded drug needles. In this part of town, they never bothered to clean up the streets. It was a waste of time. As if he sensed Drake's presence, he turned towards the alley. The neon glow revealed dark, hooded eyes and a scar that ran from cheek to chin. It was Jaeger! Drake thought he would never see him again. He hoped he wouldn't. His muttered curse was the only sound on the abandoned street. No good could come of this.*

Can you see the blue glow and feel the tension in Drake? That is the point. Show the scene to the reader, don't tell them what the character is feeling.

There are a few things to remember when it comes to details. It is important to be intentional when you are in detail mode. You want to create the illusion of reality, not reality itself. **Too many details can kill the moment and be a distraction.** Glossing over important details can slip a scene into telling mode and make it devoid of emotion. It is best to use the sharpest, most accurate details you can. Make them clear and precise. Remember:

- Too much detail kills emotion.
- Not enough detail kills emotion.
- Specific, meaningful details create emotion.
- Getting the right balance of detail comes with time and practice.

Write a fictional paragraph using detail mode:

Dialogue Mode:

Speech is powerful. All you have to do is look at politics or social media to understand that words can incite a myriad of reactions. Good or bad, what people say matters.

Dialogue is a powerful tool in the hands of an author. You can give insight into the past, give pertinent details, reveal a person's character and motives, and foreshadow danger, all within a single statement. However, to wield this powerful tool, you must understand some basic tips for writing good dialogue.

According to the NY Book Editors organization, what makes dialogue believable is **striking a balance between what you might hear in real life and an artistic rendition of a conversation.** Start listening to public conversations happening around you (without being creepy, of course). Listen to actual dialogue when real people are talking. Actual dialogue varies greatly from what new authors tend to produce in their stories. That being said, I am not asking you to replicate real-life conversations. Remember, you want the illusion of reality. It's a balance.

The following are five tips for writing good dialogue:

DO AWAY WITH PLEASANTRIES

Cutting greetings and other small talk is a great way to pare down your dialogue. If you omit all the hellos and goodbyes, you get your characters in the scene faster and allow them to tell your story through language and action. Where greetings are necessary, consider the way people would actually talk. Most people do not say "Hello" unless they are answering the phone or it is a formal setting. It's more like "Hey" if they are familiar and "Hi" if it were a surprise, awkward meeting.

KEEP THEM INVOLVED

Having only one contribution to a conversation shouldn't mean a character only speaks once. Maybe Frank's only job is to tell George when the cops pull up outside a convenience store. "The cops are here" is the only thing you need Frank for, but make sure he isn't silent until the moment he delivers that all-important line. Take the time to establish each character in the conversation and allow him to do more than just advance the plot. A discussion between two characters can do a lot for tone and character development, too.

STICK TO SIMPLE DIALOGUE TAGS

At some point in a writing class, you were no doubt told to be descriptive. When it comes to speech tags, we all spend time trying to insert creative tags like "David joked" and "Mary asked uncertainly." In general, however, descriptive speech tags distract from the real story happening within the dialogue. In general, stick to "he said" or "she said," which blends into the page and lets the reader stay in the scene. There are times to use more descriptive tags but keep them to a minimum.

DRESS YOUR DIALOGUE IN ACTION

Your dialogue creates a scene, but it doesn't have to do all the work on its own. When the "he said" or "she said" is getting dull and looking a little cluttered, omit the speech tag altogether and replace it with an action. For example:

> *"The cops are here!" Mary darted to the back of the convenience store just as Frank snatched the bag from the cashier.*

Ultimately, the only surefire way to create strong dialogue—and set your work apart—is to practice. A lot. Read your scenes with dialogue aloud; if it doesn't roll off your tongue, fiddle with it until it does. You'll hear the difference when your characters' conversations start working for you.

Let's talk a bit more about dialogue tags. Dialogue tags serve two functions: they indicate who is speaking in written dialogue and action related to the comment. Dialogue tags are essential, but there are some guides on how to use them wisely. They can enhance your story or be a tremendous distraction.

First, dispense with the myth that you need to tag every single verbal statement that characters make. If the conversation is between two people and that is indicated, you can go back and forth several times with no tag if you let the reader know at the start of the conversation who is speaking.

For example:

> Meredith closed the door of her room behind her and was surprised to see Daniel at the window staring down into the courtyard.
>
> "What do you think you are doing in here?"
>
> "We need to talk," he replied without turning around.
>
> "I cannot imagine anything you would have to say that would interest me. I have made myself clear." She walked to her desk and shuffled a few papers about, anything to keep herself from looking at him.
>
> "It is my responsibility to look after you until your father returns."
>
> "Then speak your piece and leave me be."
>
> "You cannot go to the ceremony tomorrow with the Earl of Carrington."
>
> "Why ever not?"
>
> "Because he plans to kill you."

In this example, you see minimal tags once the speaker's identity is established. They are only then used to emphasize or give context to the dialogue. With dialogue tags, less is definitely more. Just use the minimum needed.

Do not think that you have to use creative words all the time, either. Those can have a negative effect on your reader. **Most often, you will just use the tag "said" with dialogue.** The reason is this; dialogue tags can interrupt the flow of text. That is a good interruption when you want the reader to take notice, like when someone demands instead of just says something. The tag tells you the mood or emotion of the situation. But too many tags are just too many interruptions as the reader must interpret the word's meaning and relation to the scene.

The word "said" is so commonplace that readers see it without really registering it. Their brain notes who is talking but does not slow them down to consider the word's meaning.

Dialogue tags can come either before or after a statement. They can also be sandwiched in between to indicate movement or a pause or to break up long dialogue.

For example:

> "You are always so quick to jump to conclusions about me. It does not seem to matter what I do to prove that I am an asset to this team. Will you always see me as the little girl that used to tag along behind you after school?" She asked. "That is not fair, and you know it. They were my family too, and now they're gone. I want revenge just the same as everyone else!"

Like the example above, you can use tags sandwiched between dialogue, even in short dialogue sequences.

Notice the punctuation:

> "I know," she whispers, "me too."

Formatting dialogue is important. **Dialogue will always go on a new line when a different person is speaking.** You can use dialogue inside a paragraph if the paragraph is not too long; otherwise, the dialogue will get lost. Here are a few quick notes about formatting dialogue:

- The punctuation goes inside the quotes, and if the dialogue tag follows that, you do not capitalize the tag, and you punctuate afterward.
- If the tag is before the statement, then use a comma and capitalize the dialogue.
- If the tag is at the end, use a comma at the end of the statement, even if it seems like a complete sentence.

If you want to have a more in-depth review on dialogue, there are many free resources online for you to research.

Write a fictional scene using both dialogue and summary (telling) modes:

Adverbs

Adjectives and adverbs… the death of every great story. Using these even a little too much absolutely SCREAMS beginner author. Which is unfortunate when it is easily avoidable. From grade-school grammar lessons, everyone is taught that an adjective describes a noun, and an adverb describes a verb. There are lists all over the internet for both. Adverbs generally, but not always, end in -ly.

It is important to understand that what might be good for grammar class is not necessarily good for fiction writing. In fact, it's bad. **Instead of enhancing a word or sentence, these modifiers distract from the strength of a sentence.** Look at this example:

I ran quickly through the lush green grass

If this sentence were in any novel I was reading, I would roll my eyes. I mean, you're running. Is there another kind but "quickly?" Let's try again:

I ran through the grass

Better. Why? Because it already assumes that if you are running, it is quick, and all grass is pretty much green. Duh?!! People understand basic nouns without you having to expand on them.

Although rare, there may be instances in which you will need to modify a noun with an adjective, especially when the noun is outside of normal. If the grass in the sentence above was black, then that is definitely not what I would have envisioned, and, therefore, modification is necessary. The scene may have been after a fire, and that would blacken any surviving grass. That makes sense. This is the exception to the rule.

Verbs should not need modification in fiction writing… ever. Never. Ever. An adverb is just a word that points to a weak verb. In the sentence above, if you don't feel that "I ran" conveys exactly what you mean, forcing you to modify it, then forget the adverb and, instead, choose a stronger verb. How about this:

I sprinted through the grass

Although you generally want to stick with simple, straightforward language in your writing, this example is not about selecting an elaborate word that is hard to spell, harder to pronounce, and impossible to understand. This is about using **strong literary language that is accurate and direct.**

If you find you have modifiers in your story, delete them and find a stronger verb. How? By selecting the strongest verb to convey not just the action but the emphasis of that action. I am a huge fan of using a thesaurus. Just remember not to choose the most complicated word but the one that conveys the best emphasis for what you want your reader to envision.

Clichés

There is a time and a place for everything. Unfortunately, in young authors, there is a tendency to fall into the use of clichés. The problem is that they don't often know when they are doing it. In this section, we will explore this topic because it can drastically alter your reader's experience.

First, it is important to understand its meaning:

> Cliché- a phrase or opinion that is overused and betrays a lack of original thought.

I don't want to get on my reader's soapbox here, but I must tell you this is my biggest issue in genre fiction writing. In my opinion, it tends to plague the romance and Christian fiction genres primarily.

At the start, we discussed how there is nothing new when it comes to a story plot. Every plot has been written before, and that is why you must give readers something they expect but in an unexpected way. A plot that is cliché is one in which you give them something they expect exactly how they expect it. The same can be said for a clichéd character. Too often, heroes are big, strong, handsome, brave, funny, respected, rich, blah, blah... puke. Sorry, was I being too honest there? When we talked about characters in Chapter Three, we talked about writing a character that people can relate to. Well, people have flaws.

An author that falls into cliché writing is often just writing what they are familiar with or think is expected. You must avoid clichés. Think back to Chapter Two when we worked through coming up with a premise for your story. The lesson was to write what was expected and then flip it over and deliver something completely different. The process of avoiding clichés is the same if you find yourself falling into them.

I mentioned that I despise clichés, right? Just making sure I expressed myself clearly. A book that has too many clichés in the first few chapters is probably going to get slammed closed and put aside forever. Avoid them by looking for anywhere in your story that you are falling into the trap of a stereotype. It indicates lazy writing. **Be active in everything you write, think about it, question it, flip it around, write it, and then move on.**

Let's make sure you can recognize clichés when you see or read them. We will do a little exercise that will get you thinking about clichés.

Thinking of movies or books you have read, make a list of clichéd plot lines or character

Select one of these clichéd plots or characters and made some adjustments to make it unique (remember the unexpected or relatable.):

Passive Voice

Probably everyone's least favorite and hardest to understand narrative problem is the passive voice. It is the hardest for me to catch, and I still do it more often than I would like to admit. **Bear with me on this grammar portion. I know it's not the fun part, but it is necessary, and you need to learn this.**

The passive voice is something that the literary community heavily frowns upon because it causes ambiguity. Let's look at what that means. According to the UNC Writing Center, a passive construction occurs when you make the object of an action into the subject of a sentence. Whoever or whatever is performing the action is not the grammatical subject of the sentence. Look at this passive rephrasing of a familiar joke:

> Why was the road crossed by the chicken?

What is doing the action in this sentence? The chicken is the one doing the action in this sentence, but the chicken is not in the spot where you would expect the grammatical subject to be. Instead, the road is the grammatical subject. The more familiar phrasing, "Why did the chicken cross the road?" puts the actor in the subject position, the position of doing something; the chicken (the actor/ doer) crosses the road (the object). We use active verbs to represent "doing," whether it be crossing roads, proposing ideas, making arguments, or invading houses.

Once you know what to look for, passive constructions are easy to spot. Look for a form of "to be" (is, are, am, was, were, has been, have been, had been, will be, will have been, being) followed by a past participle. The past participle is a form of the verb that typically, but not always, ends in "-ed." Some exceptions to the "-ed" rule are words like "paid" (not "payed") and "driven" (not "drived").

Here's a sure-fire formula for identifying the passive voice:

Form of "to be" + past participle = passive voice

For example:

> The drawbridge <u>has been</u> scorched by the dragon's fiery breath.
>
> He <u>was walking</u> down the street minding his own business.

Need more help to decide whether a sentence is passive? Ask yourself whether there is an action going on in the sentence. If so, what is at the beginning of the sentence? Is it the person or thing that is doing the action? Or is it the person or thing that has the action done to it? In a passive sentence, the object of the action will be in the subject position at the front of the sentence.

As discussed above, the sentence will also contain a form of be and a past participle. If the subject appears at all, it will usually be at the end of the sentence, often in a phrase that starts with "by." Look at this example:

The fish was caught by the seagull.

Ask yourself if there's an action. Yes, a fish is being caught. Then, ask yourself what's at the front of the sentence, the actor or the object of the action? It's the object; the fish. Unfortunately for him, he was caught, and there it is at the front of the sentence. Now, notice that the thing that did the catching, the seagull, is at the end, after "by." There's a form of be (was) and a past participle (caught). This sentence is passive.

Let's briefly look at how to change passive constructions into active ones. You can usually just switch the word order, making the actor and subject one by putting the actor up front:

The drawbridge has been scorched by the dragon's fiery breath.

Now becomes:

The dragon scorched the drawbridge with his fiery breath.

To repeat, the key to identifying the passive voice is to look for both a form of "to be" and a past participle, which usually, but not always, ends in "-ed."

To recap passive voice identifiers:

> To Be + past participle = "Why was the road crossed by the chicken?"
>
> To Be + present participle = "He was standing." "They were walking."
>
> To Have + auxiliary to be + participle = "She had been leaning."

What is the best way to fix this? By simply changing the subject to the person doing the action.

> Passive - "He was standing at the bus stop wondering if he should have just called a cab."
>
> Active - "He paced at the bus stop wondering if he should have just called a cab."

Where I find myself making the error most often is with the To Be + present participle (he was standing) passive statements. I understand that using a passive voice is common when we speak, and training our internal editor to catch them will not be easy.

Why should you stop using a passive voice? Does it even matter?

Consider these things:

- The passive voice can reveal a weak verb. Like an adverb, it indicates that you have not chosen the best verb, and this does not help engage your reader.
- The passive voice *tells* when it means to *show*. It creates ambiguity rather than specificity and dulls the meaning of your sentence.
- The passive voice always fails to convey simultaneous actions.

OK, you did it! I know this section was dry and not as much fun as others, but this is an important part of learning to write well. You get one shot at self-publishing your first story; it is best to get it right. The good thing is that free services like Grammarly will catch a lot of this for you. You still need to understand it, but there is automated help out there.

Writing Your Story | CHAPTER SIX

Writing the Draft

By the time you come to the point of actually writing your first draft, you will have done so much planning and research that you are probably ready to get started. Perhaps the ideas and words are ready to spill out, and you are thinking, "Finally!" Because you don't have to worry about the road map of the specifics you need to cover in your story, you can just write your creative heart out. No one has to see your first draft, so don't worry.

My advice here? **Don't think. Just write.** Author Anne Lamott says it in a very relatable way, "the first draft is the child's draft, where you let it all pour out and then let it romp all over the place, knowing that no one is going to see it and that you can shape it later." Don't worry if your narration or dialogue are imperfect or don't make complete sense; you'll fix that later too. Right now, you're working on a rough draft. Just get that story out of your imagination and onto the page without being self-conscious about it.

Keep that first draft as tight as possible. You're writing a short story, after all, so be economical with your words.

- You don't need to explain everything. Give enough explanation, so the reader understands what's happening in a scene, but don't slow them down with paragraphs of backstory and exposition.

- Keep the ending in mind. As you write, determine whether each sentence ultimately progresses the plot. If it doesn't, either cut it or rework it, so it *does* progress the plot.

- Listen to how people speak. Then, write dialogue that sounds like real conversations. These conversations won't necessarily be grammatically correct, but they will make your characters sound the way people naturally speak.

Once you have a finished first draft, let it rest. If you have the luxury of waiting a day or so to come back and read what you wrote, do that. That way, you can read your writing again with fresh eyes, which makes it easier to spot inconsistencies and plot holes.

Your Internal Editor

Years of spelling lessons, grammar worksheets, and research papers with red marks all over them have honed our internal editor to some degree or another. It is hard to break away from self-correcting. I guarantee that as you sit to write your first story draft, most of you will have this inner alarm that goes off:

Wait a minute, that doesn't sound right.

Is that a run-on sentence?

There must be a better way of saying that. Thesaurus.com?

Have I used that word too many times?

When do I need a comma again?

Those red lines under a few words are driving me nuts! MUST FIX NOW.

English teachers around the globe would chastise me for what I will tell you; your internal editor is a destructive force in creative writing! I will call it a draft monster that can throttle your creativity. If you give in to that editor and fix a misspelled word or try to fix a run-on sentence, then that editor grows and gets hungrier. Soon, you are writing your third draft of the opening scene when you should be working on the climax. Not to mention you forgot the inspired details you wanted to add to the next scene by the time you finished editing that one.

If you allow your internal editor to run rampant, then you will get a disjointed grouping of grammatically correct sweeping descriptions of a broken plot. Don't encourage your internal editor, at least not yet. There is a time for editing that comes later in the revision process. **For now, you will create. Later, you will correct.**

If you really struggle with your internal editor, try these tips to help you stop feeding the draft monster:

- Assuming you touch type (which is typing without looking at your keyboard), and everyone using a computer should change your font color to a very, very light gray or blue. Yes, you will barely see what you are writing, but you won't be able to read anything you are writing. Get it? You will just write. You will let your creativity flow naturally and fix the typos and format issues later. Naturally, don't forget to change the font color to black when you are all done with the draft. I know it's assumed you would do that, but it's like the warning label on liquid bleach telling you not to drink it. Duh, but it's there for a reason.

- Dictate your words. If you choose this route, I recommend using one of the many free voice dictators online. This is one of my favorites when I want to let it flow. Granted, you cannot speak as fast as you would conversationally, but it's far more accurate than other options. This will work great for specific scenes you are working on. Then, just cut and paste your text into your story document. Another great option, especially when you are not at your computer, is to use your cell phone's audio recorder to "write" your story and then just transcribe the scene later.

Formatting

Formatting for your short story will be very straightforward. You have a minimum count of 3,000 words. You can go over that, but if this is a collected work with others, then you will need to try to keep all the pieces at a similar length. That means a variance of no more than 300-500 words per story. That is not necessarily a rule, it's just good publishing practice for consistency.

You should have your story typed in a serif font and have your text fully edited. You should have chosen your title by now, and make sure it is included at the top of your page. There will be other information about formatting when it comes to creating the actual collection into one manuscript. That will be covered in a later chapter for those participating in that type of project. For now, just make sure that your story fits these basic guidelines, and you are all set to go to the revision stage.

This week, you will write your rough draft. Let the adventure begin!

CHAPTER SEVEN

The Revision Process

Revising your Draft

The hard part is over. You have written the draft of your first story! You did it; sit back and relax. What an accomplishment.

Now, it's time to go back and get your story ready for others to read. They say the first draft is for you, from your heart, and the second is for others, from your head. That is a good illustration. **Revision can be a lengthy process, but it is vital to the success of your story.**

I love writing. Although my life as a working, homeschooling mom did not allow me to start my writing career as early as I wanted, I still wrote short stories and took as many creative writing classes as my college offered. Additionally, I have lost count of the lengthy research papers I have had to write. I even liked those. Yes, I am weird.

Whether you love writing or not, you will have written as part of your academic education. Did you ever feel like you wrote something really well, and then a few years later, you read it again? Maybe as you are cleaning out your old schoolwork? Have you noticed that what you thought was really good writing just wasn't? I have plenty of those. I can tell which essays I spent time on in the revision process and which ones I did not.

When you wrote your draft, I told you not to think too hard, just write. Write from the heart. Now it is time to write from the head. You will go back over your story and find sentences that don't fit or could have been written better. Sometimes, scenes you wrote early on do not fit with how your story developed towards the end, or you will see that the character arc went in a different direction, and now you need to clarify the earlier parts. It could be that the voice changed, or the hero was different. Whatever changed, you will find yourself needing to revise your story.

Take the revision process very seriously. It is critical to the difference between writing a short story and writing a great short story. I understand that you probably don't want to spend that much time revising. I get it. However, I assure you that without a very thorough revision process, it will be like looking back at something you thought was good that really wasn't.

First revision: This is where you will go back to the beginning, and it will be like reading it for the first time. You will have fresh eyes and see plenty that you need to change and correct. This is where you catch your spelling mistakes and grammatical errors. The following are the steps you need to take to ensure a successful first revision:

1. Check for content. Is the story really saying what you want it to say? Do you need to change or expand any dialogue? This is a good time to go back and add some foreshadowing if you feel it is necessary for an area that does not have enough tension.

2. Look for redundant words and use a thesaurus to change them. Look for adverbs and get rid of them; replace them with a strong verb. Look for adjectives that are unnecessary. You can also use the find/replace tool to search for common adverbs like "quickly."

3. Find anything that is too clichéd and change it up.

4. Go through each paragraph carefully and check for spelling and formatting errors. Look at any incorrect punctuation, paragraphs that are too long, or run-on sentences that need to be corrected. Look for capitalization errors.

5. After you correct the things above, and this is **IMPORTANT**, you **MUST** read your story out loud to yourself. The problem is two-fold:

    a. Your brain knows what you meant to say and will sometimes fill in the blanks. When you read your chapter **OUT LOUD** word-for-word, you will hear missing or awkward phrases. **I guarantee you will find many errors this way.** Do not mistake this for reading it to yourself. Out loud is, literally, out loud. The best way? Read your story to parents or siblings. You can get their input as well as catch issues.

    b. Some words are spelled the same but pronounced differently and have different meanings. These are called homographs. You should notice them when you read out loud since you are in the moment, like reading to an audience, and will catch them easier. You will also catch homophones, words that sound alike but mean different things and are spelled differently, like their and there. And lastly, homonyms are words that are spelled the same but have different meanings. None of these will be caught by spell check, so you need to read out loud.

Technically, you should go through the revision process twice. Once when you go back over it and make corrections, and again when you read it aloud to yourself. That will help you catch additional problems.

Tips for Self-Revising

The below tips are meant to encourage you to submit the best possible final manuscript of your short story. You will get out of your story exactly what you put into it, nothing less. With that in mind, I stress again the importance of taking the revision step very seriously. I have been writing for decades. My stories and books go through two to three revisions by myself, and they then get sent to a minimum of two editors. They get laid out in the software program for printing, and then I do another final revision. Do you know that I still find some errors in the printed book that arrives after all this? There are many reasons for this that I will not go into; just trust me that there is no such thing as going through to edit and revise too many times.

I have already talked to you about reading your story out loud. That is absolutely necessary. Here are some more helpful techniques for you:

- Print it out. No matter the length of your short story, it is important to print it out. The final version will be in print, and this will help you see the writing in that light. Meaning, you will visually see the final product. This is also better to get you off the computer and away from writing your story. You can easily enter edit mode and look at your story with fresh eyes. Curl up on a couch or outdoors somewhere and read your story. Make corrections with a pen and go back to the computer to fix them.

- Edit backward. One common struggle with editing your own work is getting past your attachment to certain sentences, characters, and so on. To help combat this, try editing your story backward. Start with the last paragraph, then look at the last sentence. Make sure each sentence, then each paragraph, serves a purpose. Check that it is contributing to theme, character, or plot, and if it's not, cut it out. Also, take this backward editing approach to evaluate the sound and feeling of each sentence. You'll be less affected by the flow of your story and therefore be more critical of where you need to be.

Critique Partner

Second Revision: After you have completed the first revision process, you should take part in the second revision process; the critique partner review. **Having a critique partner is vital to your success as an author. You need a different viewpoint and opinion from yours.** This can be a parent, sibling, or friend. Your "Crit Partner" will read your story and make notes and suggestions. Here are a few things to remember about crit partner reviews:

- She is your potential audience and is reading your story with no understanding of everything that went into writing it. She has no idea of character arcs or rising conflict. She is just reading the story for the sake of a story. She is the "reader" I have been referring to throughout this workbook. So, what she says reflects what future readers may say. Appreciate her unique perspective and listen with an open mind. Remember, it does not matter if you like your book; it matters if readers like your book. That is how a writer becomes an author.

- You do NOT have to take every suggestion she gives you. Consider what she says from her perspective, remembering that she has no idea of anything to do with the story outside of what is written on the page. Where you have spent months and months crafting your story and have all the background and know your character intimately, she does not. Take her advice from her perspective and make any changes that are valid. If she tells you to change or delete a section because it's boring or too long, you need to take that seriously. If she is confused about something, it is probably confusing to someone who is not intimately acquainted with the story like you are.

- Ask her to check specifically for all the spelling and grammar issues mentioned above in the first draft review. Regardless of how hard you tried, the chances are you still missed something. Once your book is printed, it's permanent. No author wants spelling mistakes in their published story.

These revision techniques will help you polish your story. Published authors usually have editors who will do much of this for them. You, however, will have to be your own editor. The benefit of this process is that you will refine and hone your writing skills. The more revisions you do, the better writer you become.

CHAPTER EIGHT

Self-Publishing

Self-Publishing a Collection

Self-publishing is the primary option for a new author writing short stories. While you can submit them to online sources for publishing, they are usually unpaid and more for testing the waters for your future writing career. And most of those will not accept your piece; it's not personal, it's statistics. You can research online for various websites and even literary journals that accept submissions from new authors and decide if you want to pursue that option. Please note that if you want to pursue traditional publishing, you should NOT self-publish your work. Most publishers will not accept any submission that is already online somewhere else.

For most new authors, short stories are a fantastic way to get started with fictional writing, and self-publishing with Amazon's Kindle Direct Publishing (KDP) is the best option. When printing a physical copy, short stories must be collected either by one author with many stories or by many authors with a common literary thread. This can be a common genre, topic, or, in this case, students in a creative writing class.

We will not discuss much about the self-publishing process in this chapter other than to let you know the general landscape of short story self-publishing. When you finish your story and are ready to submit it for publishing, formatting guidelines will be provided to you by your instructor or the person in charge of collecting for publication.

For those students who wish to pursue writing and self-publishing a collection of their own short stories, it is very important to understand the entire process. This can also be applied to anyone who wants to start a project with their friends to self-publish a collection of short stories. Whether you want to write flash fiction, short stories, novelettes, or even novellas, the process is relatively the same.

While this curriculum gives you an overview of the process, it is a good idea to pick up a copy of a short story collection so you can get a good idea of the layout requirements. You can get them from any library or purchase them from Amazon. Seeing examples for yourself gives you a better visual to reinforce what I am telling you here. If you purchased one of these printed collections at the start of the class, as recommended, then you are ahead of the game and ready to go.

The biggest issue you will tackle with self-publishing a collection will be editing. The editing process, once the stories have been collected into one document, will be the same as when writing your own story. You will have many, many sequences of editing the text, looking for mistakes and readability, looking for layout errors, and even getting extra sets of eyes to do a visual scan of the writing to ensure a uniform layout.

It is very important for you to understand that what is provided here is a general overview of each aspect of self-publishing a collection, but it is by no means an exhaustive teaching on this topic. I strongly recommend additional research online for information that many experts have written and made available for free.

Formatting a Collection

Formatting information can be found on the Kindle Direct Publishing website. The primary information you need to know is that most of these collected works will be in a 6 x 9-inch size format and have either a soft or hard cover. The font should be a serif option like Times New Roman. It is important when collecting stories together that all pieces have the same font and layout. Each story must be formatted correctly and the same as the others.

The stories will be laid out like chapters but not labeled as "Chapter One" and "Chapter Two." Instead, they will be labeled with the title of the story in place of the chapter title and the author's name.

Stories always start on a right-facing page and will have the story title as a header. The text will begin about ⅓-way down that page below the chapter and title. You can see examples of this in any collected work or even a regular chapter book. Remember, all new stories (or chapters) will start on a right-facing page. The header is larger, may even be a different font, and sometimes has a graphic or quote below it. Just remember that there must be a uniform look throughout. Below the title and optional graphic, there is blank space, then the text begins ⅓ to ½-way down the page.

The first sentence in each new paragraph will be indented, which can differ from novel formatting. Think of short stories as essays as far as the paragraph format. Dialogue will still be treated the same, on a new line for each person speaking.

For more detailed information specific to formatting your collection, visit the KDP website and find the section for formatting your book. On the KDP website, you will be able to access something like this with specific details:

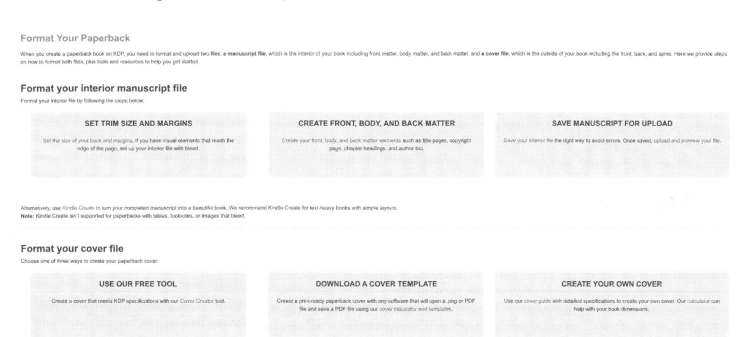

Front & Back Matter

Front matter is information about a book that comes before the main story. Front matter includes the title page, the writer's name, the edition, the publication date, the copyright details, the ISBN, and the publisher's name and logo (if applicable). It may also include a table of contents, testimonials, disclaimer, dedication, acknowledgment, contents page, a foreword, a preface, and an introduction.

Back matter is information about a book and the writer which follows the end of the main story. Back matter includes a blurb, writer biography (which may include a photo), barcode, ISBN, quotes or extracts from the book, and the publisher's name and logo. Depending on the genre, the back matter may also include an afterword, appendix, glossary, index, bibliography, and advertising about the author or publisher's other books.

There is no rule as to exactly what must be included in either front or back matter, but the commonly accepted requirements with a collection of short stories are, at minimum, front matter, including the inside title page and a table of contents.

Front Cover

The front cover for a collection of short stories will differ depending on the collection. If it is for multiple authors who write under a specific theme, one writer who has a diverse collection, or any other combination, the front cover should reflect that in the widest sense. This means that if the collection will be part of a greater collection of works, like a class of students taking creative writing, then the cover should reflect the entire effort under that identity.

Creating your own cover is very easy on KDP. There is a cover creator step that you can use with stock graphics. Additionally, you can purchase a stock image or graphic or have a friend or family member create a cover for you. The title and text for the cover can be done within the cover creator process with KDP as well.

If you want to do a completely custom cover, there are a few options. You can use a service like Fiverr.com and pay someone to create both covers and spine in the correct layout specs. Most students do not know how to use advanced design programs like Illustrator or Photoshop. That is okay; most adults don't know how to use those either. They are professional-level design tools. Not to worry, you can use simple free services like Canva to create your book cover. You will still have to come up with a spine design, but you can do that in a cover creator by uploading Canva cover artwork and using stock colors and graphics to do the back and spine.

Regardless of how you design your custom cover, there is one step that you must take first. You should download the cover template from KDP and make sure your design fits that template. This is especially important for working with a cover designer like from Fiverr. Make sure that whoever is doing your fully custom design has the correct template, or your cover upload will be rejected by KDP.

Remember that the cover is one of the most important factors when it comes to a person's reaction to your book. I always say the best advice for cover design is to go to the bookstore or the library and walk down the aisles in fiction sections. See what is popular, what you like, and, most often, the things they have consistently in common, like title placement, font sizes, cover art style, etc. Learn from those who have gone before you.

Back Cover

The back cover is where you will have the short story collection's blurb as well as a few other bits of information like the ISBN, bar code, and publishing info. The blurb, sometimes referred to as sales copy or story description, is the collection's summary so the reader understands the contents.

For a fiction novel, the blurb is the one to two-paragraph summary of a story (around 100-200 words). It typically appears on the back or dust jacket of the book. The blurb is a cross between a sales pitch and a summary. After looking at the cover of a book, the first thing a person will do is flip it over and read the blurb on the back (or scroll down the page if on Amazon or similar).

However, for a collection of short stories, the blurb will be very different. Since the stories can be very diverse and may not follow one theme, you will not follow the typical rules for writing the blurb. Instead, you will focus on enticing readers to purchase the book. Here is an example from the short story anthology called *Small Odysseys:*

> *A must-have for any lover of literature, Small Odysseys sweeps the reader into the landscape of the contemporary short story, featuring never-before-published works by many of our most preeminent authors as well as up-and-coming superstars.*
>
> *On their journey through the book, readers will encounter long-ago movie stars, a town full of dandelions, and math lessons from Siri. They will attend karaoke night, hear a twenty-something slacker's breathless report of his failed recruiting by the FBI, and travel with a father and son as they channel grief into running a neighborhood bakery truck. They will watch the Greek goddess Persephone encounter the end of the world and witness another apocalypse through a series of advertisements for a touchless bidet. And finally, they will meet an aging loner who finds courage and resilience hidden in the most unexpected of places—the next generation.*
>
> *Published in partnership with beloved literary radio program and live show Selected Shorts in honor of its thirty-fifth anniversary, this collection of thirty-five stories captures its spirit in print for the first time.*
>
> *FEATURING*
>
> *Rabih Alameddine * Jenny Allen * Lesley Nneka Arimah * Aimee Bender * Marie-Helene Bertino * Jai Chakrabarti * Patrick Cottrell * Elizabeth Crane * Michael Cunningham * Patrick Dacey * Edwidge Danticat * Dave Eggers * Omar El Akkad * Lauren Groff * Jacob Guajardo * A.M. Homes * Mira Jacob * Jac Jemc * Etgar Keret * Lisa Ko * Victor LaValle * J. Robert Lennon * Ben Loory * Carmen Maria Machado * Juan Martinez * Maile Meloy * Joe Meno * Susan Perabo * Helen Phillips * Namwali Serpell * Rivers Solomon * Elizabeth Strout * Luis Alberto Urrea * Jess Walter * Weike Wang*

In this example, the blurb includes some general concepts from multiple stories presented in an invitation to journey through the book. The authors are listed on the back cover, which is more common for well-known authors who have published works. Some blurbs for short story collections are minimalist, with only two to three sentences. I feel the blurb is important and deserves relevant attention to encourage readers to want to pick it up and read.

The Final Step

One issue that persistently plagues self-publishing is a lack of attention to detail. There has been a general disregard for producing a clean final copy that may be due to a lack of knowledge or, unfortunately, a bit of laziness at the home stretch. It takes effort here in the final steps to get it done right.

If you do not know how to self-publish a book, there are hundreds or more free resources and how-to videos available online. Again, it is well worth the effort to get it right. All the work that was put into writing the stories deserves the best production available.

Self-Publishing with KDP:

1. Collect the short stories and put them into one document with the correct layout. This will become your manuscript.
2. Create front and back matter and place into the manuscript document.
3. Design front and back cover. If using cover creator, you will do this during the upload process.
4. A free Amazon ISBN will be provided to you when you upload your manuscript, and Amazon will be listed as the publisher.
5. Visit the KDP website and take a walk through the steps to publishing with them. They are your guide for the rest of the process.

That is it! You are all set to take a fantastic journey with your fellow writers and friends. This has been an incredible journey, and you should be very proud of yourself. You worked hard for this achievement. I would bet that you worked harder than you thought you would when you first opened this workbook.

Writing fiction is a craft. It takes time and effort to develop the skill. You have taken the first major step, and I now encourage you to continue writing if this is something you enjoyed. The world is constantly evolving and moving forward, but some things never change… people love good stories.

Perhaps you are just the person to give them more?

If you are interested in writing your first fiction novel, check out our *180 Days to Save the World* curriculum at www.innovativelearningpress.com

Bonus Materials | CHAPTER NINE

Story Collection Worksheets

This workbook is written for students who want to write their own collection of short stories over one school year and self-publish the collection, or for students who are taking part in a group or class setting and will submit one story as part of a collaboration with other writers.

These bonus materials are generally for students in the former group; those who will write multiple stories and self-publish their own collection. The following pages will give you the opportunity to use worksheets and note pages to plan and outline multiple stories. There is no specific requirement for the total number of stories you must include in a collection, but KDP requires a minimum page count of 24 interior pages.

I recommend you complete a minimum of six more short stories over one school year. This curriculum is set up to take eight weeks (2 months) to complete and that gives you plenty of time to write additional stories. If you choose to write more stories for your collection, you can use this workbook as a guide and complete the planning using a blank notebook. Also, these worksheets can be fore the latter group if you just need extra sheets for your story or you want to work on an alternate plot line. Happy writing!

NOTES

NOTES

CHARACTER WORKSHEET

Character Name _____

Sketch or Paste Image

NickName _____

Physical Description

POSITIVE IDEALS

Personality

NEGATIVE IDEALS

Habits / Quirks

Goals and Motivations

Background

CHARACTER WORKSHEET

Character Name _____

Sketch or Paste Image

NickName _____

Physical Description
_____
_____
_____
_____

POSITIVE IDEALS

Personality
_____
_____
_____
_____

NEGATIVE IDEALS

Habits / Quirks
_____
_____
_____
_____

Goals and Motivations

Background
_____
_____
_____
_____

EXTERNAL SUFFERING

EVENT	SUFFERING

EVENT	SUFFERING

EVENT	SUFFERING

INTERNAL SUFFERING

| EVENT | » | SUFFERING |

| EVENT | » | SUFFERING |

| EVENT | » | SUFFERING |

CHARACTER IDEALS CHART

Character	Positive Ideals	Negative Ideals

THEME MIND MAP

1. What negative ideal does the hero start with?

2. What motivated the hero to pursue the story goal?

The hero's lesson

3. What choices did the hero make that had devastating consequences?

5. How did the hero overcome and restore the negative consequences?

4. How did the negative consequences affect the hero and the story goal?

Notes:

KEY ELEMENTS PLANNER

Goal
What does the hero want at the beginning of the story?

Conflict
What stops him from achieving his goal?

Disaster
What happens & how does the hero end up worse than before?

Reaction
What does the hero react emotionally? + or - ideals?

Dilemma
What possible options are available at the hero?

Decision
What does the hero decide to do? (what is his new path?)

KEY ELEMENTS PLANNER

Goal
What does the hero want at the beginning of the story?

Conflict
What stops him from achieving his goal?

Disaster
What happens & how does the hero end up worse than before?

Reaction
What does the hero react emotionally? + or - ideals?

Dilemma
What possible options are available at the hero?

Decision
What does the hero decide to do? (what is his new path?)

KEY EVENTS OUTLINE

Note the main events in this story.
Include general time event occurs (day/night, etc), duration (how long), location, and characters invloved.

▸

▸

▸

▸

▸

▸

▸

▸

▸

▸

▸

KEY EVENTS OUTLINE

Note the main events in this story.

Include general time event occurs (day/night, etc), duration (how long), location, and characters invloved.

›
›
›
›
›
›
›
›
›
›
›
›

NOTES

NOTES

CHARACTER WORKSHEET

Character Name _____

[Sketch or Paste Image]

NickName _____

Physical Description
_____
_____
_____
_____

POSITIVE IDEALS

Personality
_____
_____
_____
_____

NEGATIVE IDEALS

Habits / Quirks
_____
_____

Goals and Motivations

Background
_____

CHARACTER WORKSHEET

Character Name _____

Sketch or Paste Image

NickName _____

Physical Description

POSITIVE IDEALS

Personality

NEGATIVE IDEALS

Habits / Quirks

Goals and Motivations

Background

EXTERNAL SUFFERING

EVENT		SUFFERING
	»	

EVENT		SUFFERING
	»	

EVENT		SUFFERING
	»	

INTERNAL SUFFERING

EVENT		SUFFERING
	»	

EVENT		SUFFERING
	»	

EVENT		SUFFERING
	»	

CHARACTER IDEALS CHART

Character	Positive Ideals	Negative Ideals

THEME MIND MAP

1. What negative ideal does the hero start with?

2. What motivated the hero to pursue the story goal?

The hero's lesson

3. What choices did the hero make that had devastating consequences?

5. How did the hero overcome and restore the negative consequences?

4. How did the negative consequences affect the hero and the story goal?

Notes:

KEY ELEMENTS PLANNER

Goal
What does the hero want at the beginning of the story?

Conflict
What stops him from achieving his goal?

Disaster
What happens & how does the hero end up worse than before?

Reaction
What does the hero react emotionally? + or - ideals?

Dilemma
What possible options are available at the hero?

Decision
What does the hero decide to do? (what is his new path?)

KEY ELEMENTS PLANNER

Goal
What does the hero want at the beginning of the story?

Conflict
What stops him from achieving his goal?

Disaster
What happens & how does the hero end up worse than before?

Reaction
What does the hero react emotionally? + or - ideals?

Dilemma
What possible options are available at the hero?

Decision
What does the hero decide to do? (what is his new path?)

KEY EVENTS OUTLINE

Note the main events in this story.
Include general time event occurs (day/night, etc), duration (how long), location, and characters invloved.

▸

▸

▸

▸

▸

▸

▸

▸

▸

▸

▸

KEY EVENTS OUTLINE

Note the main events in this story.

Include general time event occurs (day/night, etc), duration (how long), location, and characters invloved.

-
-
-
-
-
-
-
-
-
-
-
-

NOTES

NOTES

CHARACTER WORKSHEET

Character Name _____

Sketch or Paste Image

NickName _____

Physical Description

POSITIVE IDEALS

Personality

NEGATIVE IDEALS

Habits / Quirks

Goals and Motivations

Background

CHARACTER WORKSHEET

Character Name _____

Sketch or Paste Image

NickName _____

Physical Description
_____
_____
_____
_____
_____

POSITIVE IDEALS

Personality
_____
_____
_____
_____
_____

NEGATIVE IDEALS

Habits / Quirks
_____
_____
_____
_____

Goals and Motivations

Background
_____
_____
_____
_____
_____

EXTERNAL SUFFERING

EVENT	SUFFERING

EVENT	SUFFERING

EVENT	SUFFERING

INTERNAL SUFFERING

EVENT	SUFFERING

EVENT	SUFFERING

EVENT	SUFFERING

CHARACTER IDEALS CHART

Character	Positive Ideals	Negative Ideals

THEME MIND MAP

1. What negative ideal does the hero start with?

2. What motivated the hero to pursue the story goal?

The hero's lesson

3. What choices did the hero make that had devastating consequences?

5. How did the hero overcome and restore the negative consequences?

4. How did the negative consequences affect the hero and the story goal?

Notes:

KEY ELEMENTS PLANNER

Goal
What does the hero want at the beginning of the story?

Conflict
What stops him from achieving his goal?

Disaster
What happens & how does the hero end up worse than before?

Reaction
What does the hero react emotionally? + or - ideals?

Dilemma
What possible options are available at the hero?

Decision
What does the hero decide to do? (what is his new path?)

KEY ELEMENTS PLANNER

Goal
What does the hero want at the beginning of the story?

Conflict
What stops him from achieving his goal?

Disaster
What happens & how does the hero end up worse than before?

Reaction
What does the hero react emotionally? + or - ideals?

Dilemma
What possible options are available at the hero?

Decision
What does the hero decide to do? (what is his new path?)

KEY EVENTS OUTLINE

Note the main events in this story.

Include general time event occurs (day/night, etc), duration (how long), location, and characters invloved.

-
-
-
-
-
-
-
-
-
-
-
-

KEY EVENTS OUTLINE

Note the main events in this story.

Include general time event occurs (day/night, etc), duration (how long), location, and characters invloved.

-
-
-
-
-
-
-
-
-
-
-
-

NOTES

NOTES

CHARACTER WORKSHEET

Character Name _____

Sketch or Paste Image

NickName _____

Physical Description
_____

POSITIVE IDEALS

Personality
_____

NEGATIVE IDEALS

Habits / Quirks
_____

Goals and Motivations

Background
_____

CHARACTER WORKSHEET

Character Name _____

Sketch or Paste Image

NickName _____

Physical Description
_____
_____
_____
_____

POSITIVE IDEALS

Personality
_____
_____
_____
_____

NEGATIVE IDEALS

Habits / Quirks
_____
_____
_____

Goals and Motivations

Background
_____
_____
_____

EXTERNAL SUFFERING

EVENT	SUFFERING
EVENT	SUFFERING
EVENT	SUFFERING

INTERNAL SUFFERING

| EVENT | » | SUFFERING |

| EVENT | » | SUFFERING |

| EVENT | » | SUFFERING |

CHARACTER IDEALS CHART

Character	Positive Ideals	Negative Ideals

THEME MIND MAP

1. What negative ideal does the hero start with?

2. What motivated the hero to pursue the story goal?

The hero's lesson

3. What choices did the hero make that had devastating consequences?

5. How did the hero overcome and restore the negative consequences?

4. How did the negative consequences affect the hero and the story goal?

Notes:

KEY ELEMENTS PLANNER

Goal
What does the hero want at the beginning of the story?

Conflict
What stops him from achieving his goal?

Disaster
What happens & how does the hero end up worse than before?

Reaction
What does the hero react emotionally? + or - ideals?

Dilemma
What possible options are available at the hero?

Decision
What does the hero decide to do? (what is his new path?)

KEY ELEMENTS PLANNER

Goal
What does the hero want at the beginning of the story?

Conflict
What stops him from achieving his goal?

Disaster
What happens & how does the hero end up worse than before?

Reaction
What does the hero react emotionally? + or - ideals?

Dilemma
What possible options are available at the hero?

Decision
What does the hero decide to do? (what is his new path?)

KEY EVENTS OUTLINE

Note the main events in this story.

Include general time event occurs (day/night, etc), duration (how long), location, and characters invloved.

-
-
-
-
-
-
-
-
-
-
-
-

KEY EVENTS OUTLINE

Note the main events in this story.
Include general time event occurs (day/night, etc), duration (how long), location, and characters invloved.

›
›
›
›
›
›
›
›
›
›
›

NOTES

NOTES

CHARACTER WORKSHEET

Character Name _____

Sketch or Paste Image

NickName _____

Physical Description
_____
_____
_____
_____

POSITIVE IDEALS

Personality
_____
_____
_____

NEGATIVE IDEALS

Habits / Quirks
_____
_____

Goals and Motivations

Background
_____
_____

CHARACTER WORKSHEET

Character Name _____

Sketch or Paste Image

NickName _____

Physical Description
_____
_____
_____
_____

POSITIVE IDEALS

Personality
_____
_____
_____
_____

NEGATIVE IDEALS

Habits / Quirks
_____
_____
_____

Goals and Motivations

Background
_____
_____
_____
_____

EXTERNAL SUFFERING

EVENT	SUFFERING
EVENT	SUFFERING
EVENT	SUFFERING

INTERNAL SUFFERING

EVENT	SUFFERING

EVENT	SUFFERING

EVENT	SUFFERING

CHARACTER IDEALS CHART

Character	Positive Ideals	Negative Ideals

THEME MIND MAP

1. What negative ideal does the hero start with?

2. What motivated the hero to pursue the story goal?

The hero's lesson

3. What choices did the hero make that had devastating consequences?

5. How did the hero overcome and restore the negative consequences?

4. How did the negative consequences affect the hero and the story goal?

Notes:

KEY ELEMENTS PLANNER

Goal
What does the hero want at the beginning of the story?

Conflict
What stops him from achieving his goal?

Disaster
What happens & how does the hero end up worse than before?

Reaction
What does the hero react emotionally? + or - ideals?

Dilemma
What possible options are available at the hero?

Decision
What does the hero decide to do? (what is his new path?)

KEY ELEMENTS PLANNER

Goal
What does the hero want at the beginning of the story?

Conflict
What stops him from achieving his goal?

Disaster
What happens & how does the hero end up worse than before?

Reaction
What does the hero react emotionally? + or - ideals?

Dilemma
What possible options are available at the hero?

Decision
What does the hero decide to do? (what is his new path?)

KEY EVENTS OUTLINE

Note the main events in this story.
Include general time event occurs (day/night, etc), duration (how long), location, and characters invloved.

▸
▸
▸
▸
▸
▸
▸
▸
▸
▸
▸
▸

KEY EVENTS OUTLINE

Note the main events in this story.

Include general time event occurs (day/night, etc), duration (how long), location, and characters invloved.

-
-
-
-
-
-
-
-
-
-
-
-

NOTES

NOTES

CHARACTER WORKSHEET

Character Name _____

Sketch or Paste Image

NickName _____

Physical Description
_____
_____
_____
_____

POSITIVE IDEALS

Personality
_____
_____
_____
_____

NEGATIVE IDEALS

Habits / Quirks
_____
_____

Goals and Motivations

Background
_____

CHARACTER WORKSHEET

Character Name _____

Sketch or Paste Image

NickName _____

Physical Description
_____
_____
_____
_____
_____

POSITIVE IDEALS

Personality
_____
_____
_____
_____
_____

NEGATIVE IDEALS

Habits / Quirks
_____
_____
_____
_____

Goals and Motivations

Background
_____
_____
_____
_____

EXTERNAL SUFFERING

EVENT	SUFFERING

EVENT	SUFFERING

EVENT	SUFFERING

INTERNAL SUFFERING

EVENT	SUFFERING
EVENT	SUFFERING
EVENT	SUFFERING

CHARACTER IDEALS CHART

Character	Positive Ideals	Negative Ideals

THEME MIND MAP

1. What negative ideal does the hero start with?

2. What motivated the hero to pursue the story goal?

The hero's lesson

3. What choices did the hero make that had devastating consequences?

5. How did the hero overcome and restore the negative consequences?

4. How did the negative consequences affect the hero and the story goal?

Notes:

KEY ELEMENTS PLANNER

Goal
What does the hero want at the beginning of the story?

Conflict
What stops him from achieving his goal?

Disaster
What happens & how does the hero end up worse than before?

Reaction
What does the hero react emotionally? + or - ideals?

Dilemma
What possible options are available at the hero?

Decision
What does the hero decide to do? (what is his new path?)

KEY ELEMENTS PLANNER

Goal
What does the hero want at the beginning of the story?

Conflict
What stops him from achieving his goal?

Disaster
What happens & how does the hero end up worse than before?

Reaction
What does the hero react emotionally? + or - ideals?

Dilemma
What possible options are available at the hero?

Decision
What does the hero decide to do? (what is his new path?)

KEY EVENTS OUTLINE

Note the main events in this story.

Include general time event occurs (day/night, etc), duration (how long), location, and characters invloved.

▸

▸

▸

▸

▸

▸

▸

▸

▸

▸

▸

KEY EVENTS OUTLINE

Note the main events in this story.
Include general time event occurs (day/night, etc), duration (how long), location, and characters invloved.

-
-
-
-
-
-
-
-
-
-
-
-

PARTING THOUGHTS

This has been an incredible journey and you should be very proud of yourself. You worked hard for this achievement. I would bet that you worked a lot harder than you thought you would when you first opened this workbook.

Writing fiction is a craft. It takes time and effort to develop the skill. You have taken the first major step and now I encourage you to continue writing if this is something you enjoyed. The world is constantly evolving and moving forward but some things never change... people love good stories.

Perhaps you are just the person to give them more?

With affection,

jg

ABOUT THE AUTHOR

Jane Garrett is the pen name for Sarah Reid. Why a pen name? Not to have a secret identity or escape a life of crime. No, her pen name is much more personal.

Sarah chose that name many years ago when she dreamed of becoming a full-time author. She wanted her author's persona to reflect the family effort it takes to support someone who chooses a career in writing. Her mom, also her biggest fan, lost her battle with breast cancer in 2012. Sarah and her mom share the same middle name, Jane. Her amazing husband, Captain Awesome, also known as Garrett to mere mortals, encouraged her for many years to pursue this path. Patience is his superpower. Sarah is now a full-time author and Jane Garrett represents the support system that helped get her there.

Sarah obtained her BA in Organizational Management from Ashford University and her MA in Writing from Johns Hopkins University. She homeschooled her two children through high school graduation before sending them off to college.

Sarah taught high school in the private sector for five years and went on to become the director of Eden Learning Academy for three years until March 2020. Since that time, she has written six curriculum books and started her own publishing company, Innovative Learning Press. As an author and teacher, Jane Garrett is passionate about helping students be involved and intentional when making choices for their future. Her writing focuses on helping students find their own passion for learning

OTHER BOOKS BY JANE GARRETT

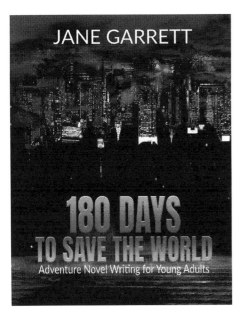

180 Days to Save the World: Adventure Novel Writing for Young Adults

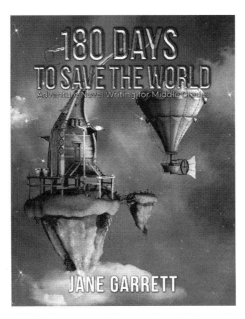

180 Days to Save the World: Adventure Novel Writing for Middle Grades

Travel Learn Create Travelschool Workbook

The Encephalon Code: Level 1 Student Workbook

The Encephalon Code: Level 2 Student Workbook

The Encephalon Code: Level 3 Student Workbook

Made in the USA
Columbia, SC
13 June 2023

17840321R00113